EXPRESSIONS IN RHYME

Edited by

Natalie Nightingale

First published in Great Britain in 2002 by
POETRY NOW
Remus House,
Coltsfoot Drive,
Peterborough, PE2 9JX
Telephone (01733) 898101
Fax (01733) 313524

HB ISBN 0 75432 754 X
SB ISBN 0 75432 755 8

FOREWORD

Although we are a nation of poets we are accused of not reading poetry, or buying poetry books. After many years of listening to the incessant gripes of poetry publishers, I can only assume that the books they publish, in general, are books that most people do not want to read.

Poetry should not be obscure, introverted, and as cryptic as a crossword puzzle: it is the poet's duty to reach out and embrace the world.

The world owes the poet nothing and we should not be expected to dig and delve into a rambling discourse searching for some inner meaning.

The reason we write poetry (and almost all of us do) is because we want to communicate: an ideal; an idea; or a specific feeling. Poetry is as essential in communication, as a letter; a radio; a telephone, and the main criterion for selecting the poems in this anthology is very simple: they communicate.

CONTENTS

RED KITES AT RHAYADER

Out of the distant hills they came
High o'er the valleys on wings of flame;
Circling and soaring, higher and higher
High o'er the valleys on wings of fire.

Bright in the sunlight, high o'er the trees,
Tumbling and swooping with effortless ease,
Down from the mountains, red wings a-quiver
Follow the valley, hang o'er the river.

Fabled in legend, fierce-eyed, forked tails,
Red kites, proudly returned now to Wales.

Wendy Teale

I HAVE A MISSION

I have a mission coupled with a vision
Sure it's a mission and never an illusion
With all submission and yes, a contribution
Beyond imagination, here crops up the solution
And with determination, it comes to fruition
To all oppressions, I will suppress
I will never be entangled in a mess
I shall come through no matter the stress
Forward ever, I shall know no recess
With all courage, I will accomplish my quest
Together with hope and faith, bringing out my best
Till it is done, never on my oars shall I rest
I will fulfil my quest, whether or not abounds a test
Success the aftermath, it shall know no bounds
I will take care of the pennies, they will do,
                        themselves, the pounds
It's up to me to move, seeing if He moves with me
In accomplishing my mission, help, it's only he
No matter the setbacks, that come my way, day to day
I depend on my Lord, everyday I pray
Waiting for a response, keeping me at bay
Then it shall come and sure it shall show me the way
Whether in broad daylight or even in the night
The road I'd take would be right, suffering no plight
Then I shall proclaim, I had a mission
And with dedication, it has come to fruition.

Ato Ulzen-Appiah

WHERE IS MY KINGDOM NOW?

Long ago, I slipped from a boat
Into a shoreless, polished sea
And floated there, like driftwood,
While a coppered sun flamed down on me.
Indigo water flounced about,
Caressed my body as I lay.
I looked through my maybug spectacles -
And entered a kingdom worlds away.

Slowly and silently I slid
Through halls with floors of palest gold
And rosy walls where molluscs clung
In houses that were whorled and scrolled.
Crustaceans paddled soundlessly,
Humping sea chests on their backs
And piscine figures cruised and sculled
Through forests marked with glistening tracks.

And now? Where is my kingdom now?
The tanker has spewed the sludge and the slob
That slimed those waters and clogged those halls,
That wrenched the last silent scream and sob
From each living thing that could not flee,
Choking as it fought for breath,
Gasping in its agony,
Dragged to its slow, malignant death.

And a grey creeps over me as I brood,
For I know the when, the why and the how
That answers the question I ask again -
And again, 'Where is my kingdom now?'

Patricia Lewis

THE RIVER TEES

As I stand and look to the mouth of the Tees,
My face is cold, as I feel the breeze.
My cheek is wet from the spray of the sea,
My heart lies here, for this is home to me.

The ships they came from far and wide,
They journeyed the river, to the busy dockside.
All manner of ships came from the sea,
It was not just a life but an industry.

Iron and steel was exported afar,
To foreign lands miles apart.
Then the ships they stopped, they came no more,
For a dark time had come, we went to war.

She survived the war and lived again,
But was defeated by recession caused by man.
Factories closed, industry died,
The ships then stopped, there was an empty tide.

As I stand and look to the mouth of the Tees,
I begin to falter as I feel the breeze.
As I turn my back and walk away,
I know in my heart, she's had her day.

Andrew Brian Zipfell

REAL LOVE

Seasons come and seasons go
There is a reason - this we know
But in our hearts we still ask why
Why do our loved ones have to die?

A mum, a daughter, a sister and wife
You gave us so much of your life
It's oh so clear now that you've gone
That for you we must be strong

Flowers come up fresh and bright
In the sunny morning light
Then after the pleasure they bring is done
They fade away in the evening sun

Some flowers last and never die
But they are not real - that is why
Real love and beauty does not last
It is strong at first but fades so fast

Then too late we realise
All the love you had inside
The love you shared with everyone
The laughter you shared - you were such fun!

Cheered everyone who came your way
The day you died was oh so grey
So when the seasons come and go
We remember how much we love you so.

Tricia Layton

THE CHARITY SHOP

Oh what a wonderful place to browse
To try on trousers, a skirt or blouse,
See second-hand books, lots of old magazines
Cutlery, crockery, old sewing machines.

Ties and belts and pictures for walls,
Football and rugger shirts, bats and balls,
Candlesticks, dishes, saucepans and mugs,
Quite a selection of fancy jugs.

Underwear, outerwear, jackets and macks,
Old fashioned ornaments, some with cracks,
Pillowslips, sheets and blankets galore
All there to gather cash for the poor.

I gazed and I wonder, what tales they could tell
For there's a story behind everything they sell
I just can't pass by, I just have to stop,
To browse and look around that old charity shop.

Cyril Storer

TOM CAT

Tom Cat loved to laze and stretch out in the morning sun,
But if another cat came near he could get up and run.
He'd chase cats whether they were large or small,
He'd see them off over the garden wall.
Then one day a tiny black kitten appeared.
It was brought by a man with a long dark beard.
Tom's mistress had a fit of 'oohs' and 'ahs'.
She didn't shout when it knocked over a vase.
Tom hid and watched through the patio window,
Waiting for the moment when the kitten would go.
Tom's mistress went into the hall to use the phone.
The kitten was left in the lounge on its own.
Tom decided that now was the time to show himself,
He startled the kitten who fell off the shelf.
It hissed at Tom as it arched its back,
It went over to Tom who tried to give it a whack.
The patio window was closed but then
That didn't stop Tom trying to whack it again.
The kitten decided that enough was enough,
Yes, now was the time for it to get tough.
It hurled itself at the window with full force.
The glass put a stop to it of course.
Just then Tom's mistress returned and was shocked.
She turned the key in the window, which was locked.
She picked up the kitten and took it outside with her.
'Silly kitten the window was shut, take more care.'
Tom Cat lay stretched out in the morning sun,
His mistress hadn't seen what he'd done.
He'd be able to try again another day,
He'd make sure that kitten didn't stay.

Rosina L Gutcher

TOTAL REDEMPTION

Cut up, spun out, turned around!
Intuition hits destination!
Fear introduces new vibration!
A clear-cut new conception!
A clear view love perception!
There's only one way to perfection!
Total redemption!

Vincent Rees

SPRING

Daffodils are blowing in the breeze
Birds are singing in the trees
Baby lambs just newly born
Mothers by them in the field - just shorn
Spring is here all things anew
Snowdrops in the morning dew
Blackbirds singing in the bush
Making nests 'longside a thrush
Soon the evenings will be light
Well into the early night
Springtime is a lovely season
Leaving winter behind - that's the reason!
Enjoy the months of pretty flowers
While away the leisurely hours
Nice walks along the sands
Strolling together holding hands
Nature at its very best
Baby birds are in their nest
This is the nicest time of year
With everything we hold most dear.

Brownie

IDEALS IN RHYME

A calm, secluded place to fish
A dark, green wood to walk
An inglenook with logs aglow
Just meeting friends to talk

Never-ending Christmas Eves
Soft rain upon my face
A royal flush at poker
Horses I back win every race

Self cleaning shoes with soles that last
Socks that always stay in pairs
My car to run on H^2O
Someone to decorate my stairs

A pen that's always full of ink
Blank papers when I need them
A brain to finding the words that rhyme
And spells so I can read 'em!

Toast that falls with dryside down
Lawn grass that needs no mowing
A video that tapes on time
A credit balance that keeps growing

A life of ease and luxury
A family that cares
Some words to end this poem
Oh well - it's off to bed upstairs!

Roy Smith

WEST END WINNER

(Dedicated to Louise Plowright -
for leading the West End show, 'Mamma Mia')

A show's leading lady
Has to be capable.
The show she must carry,
And yet she must rule;
What'er the others be
As *The Winner Takes It All:*
Co-stars who act badly,
Or a scene-stealer's call.

If the supports are weak,
She'll lead them like a kite.
But if they can compete,
Then she'll give them a fight.
Audience in their seat
See her star shining bright.
Who can rise to this feat?
Just watch *Louise Plowright.*

Emma Dorothy Shane

BELIEVE IT OR NOT!

I went for a breath of fresh air -
When I was out, I met a bear -
I really did not seem to care -
Had someone fixed for me a dare?

I jumped on a bus and paid my fare,
Sat down quickly, combed my hair,
Passed a fox leaving his lair -
Next a field, a lovely grey mare.

Orchards to follow - I longed for a pear,
But bus stops really were quite rare.
I took a jump, caught dress, heard a tear
Now I was naked - nothing to wear!

Next I woke up!
Morning tea in a cup.
What a relief!
T'was beyond belief!

Cindy White

OUR LOVE

What brings the joy to your heart,
Flowers, blooming like some art.

What brings the smile on your face,
Because you are a part of a human race.

What makes me want to hold you tight,
Together, this is for our future bright.

What make me want to put the ring
On your finger, and let our love linger.

A Bhambra

SPOILT FOR CHOICE

Have you thought about all the choices
We have in our lives each day?
What to wear, and what to eat,
Where to go and where to stay!

We now have clothes for every occasion,
Trouser suits, minis and leisurewear
Anoraks, trainers, jeans and long-johns
What choice - what colours - to share!

What about holidays - home or abroad,
The thing we can't choose - is the weather
Don't let that worry you - there's these Center Parcs
With Jacuzzis, wave machines, pools - whatever!

Then there's the food, spoilt for choice in the shops
For variety of cheeses and meats,
Yoghurts, fruit, veggies and bread
So many different kinds of treats.

Choice of life-style, married or single,
One parent families can be planned
Live-in lovers or communal kibbutz
Nothing is sacred - and nothing is banned!

Win Forster

MY SCINTILLATING DREAM

My dream last night enthralled me,
'Twas one of ecstasy.
I floated up to plains on high,
Just for myself, to see.
The picture that unfolded,
Was beyond my wildest dreams.
I'd ended in some wonderland,
With love bursting at its seams.
Where everyone had golden hair,
Blue eyes, angelic face.
No sign of mortal hatred here,
This was a super place.
Alas it ended when I awoke,
To find of love, such dearth.
Because my scintillating dream,
Had taken place - on Earth.

Jack Blades

THE LAWN

'Tis said that '10 men went to mow' -
but only one is here.
I have the floating Flymo
but the nine have gone for beer.

The grass is thick and weedy
(mainly, it is weeds!);
some stalks are thick and reedy
and the edging line recedes.

The foxes play upon it;
dogs dig for long-lost bones.
A fir tree overhangs it
and covers it with cones.

The roots of trees invade it
and send their suckers up.
The autumn leaves pervade it
and need a sweeper-up.

Worms its green may desecrate
and cast their mud upon it.
Dandelions penetrate -
their seedlings seem infinite.

Stray cattle graze upon it
and leave it less than clean.
Neighbours' cats sleep on it
When'er they choose to preen.

Day comes when all shall end their play
and I retire from work.
It's there for me to sunbathe -
wearing an owner's smirk!

Jo Allen

A SMALL COTTAGE

There is a small cottage perched on the hill
With white walls and red tiles
In all weather it stands so proud, so still
Looking around for miles

Drawing a sort of archway above the door
Amongst other shrubs grows
Adding a touch of grace to the decor
An erratic red rose

At night, windows wide awake, the valley
It surveys, while willows
In rippled mirrors, at hide and seek play
With clouds as the moon glows

Life stealthily emerges holding its breath
Sidling foxes, badgers
Silent birds swooping; they all live on death
In or out of hedges

Giving food and shelter to travellers
(All that can fly or crawl)
Springs open the gates to vivid colours
But winters bare it all

The small cottage appears to guard the hill
For miles around it's seen
It stands above the valley proud and still
Watching the changing scene.

J-C Chandenier

WAKE UP CALL

It was six in the morning
And just growing light;
The pains that consume me
Had made a long night.
Awoken by faint sounds
Which began to increase,
I was suddenly visited
By a huge skein of geese.
They circled the house
Making sure that I'd heard
The loud joyous greetings
Of this wonderful bird.
I smiled as they left me
For, dear Father, I knew
This was a reminder
Of the nearness of You.

Geraldine Laker

JUST TWO THINGS TO REMEMBER

World Trade Center, Pentagon,
Hiroshima, Omah bomb,
Dresden, Coventry, London,
Tel Aviv - the list goes on.

Freedom fighter, terrorist.
He must fight on - he must resist.
Pious churchman, politician,
United Nation resolution.

Each is convinced that he is right
Conveniently losing sight
Of the guidelines well defined -
Love God with all your heart and mind

And your neighbour as yourself.

Alf Cole

A MOTHER'S LOVE

I am a child, she loves me,
In a way only mothers can,
A safe and warm secure love,
That doesn't come so easy to man.

In teenage years she guided me,
She taught me right from wrong.
Sometimes I raved and ranted
But she knew it wouldn't last long.

She sensed if I was hurting,
Said the right things, kept me sane,
Did the things that good mums do
To take away my pain.

I am now a mother of two,
I hope I'm my children's friend,
So why after all these years Mum,
Does our closeness have to end?

I respect you have your new life,
We're all sad we lost our dear dad,
But I truly still need my 'Old Mum',
The 'New One' doesn't know when I'm sad.

Julie Tucker

NAN

I can't remember a time when you weren't there
Helping and guiding me with love and care
From an infant your love was constant and true
Now you've gone what will I do
I know you're in a much better place
When I close my eyes I see your face
A better nan no one could find
You didn't want to leave us behind
But you were tired and needed a rest
It's true what they say! God takes the best.

J Smith

MEMORY

Memory should be a pleasure,
Something we can always treasure,
So, why is it pain?
That which is gone cannot return
However much we for it yearn
And to be young again.

Careless youth that cannot know
How very quickly time will go,
Taste life while you may;
So much will not come again,
So much effort will be vain,
Enjoy each fleeting day.

Only the very old may see
The purpose of the panoply
And judge the best of it.
Never deny your heritage,
Read your every written page
And live the best of it.

Anne James

MY DUVET COVER

I woke up this morning,
It was duvet changing day,
Planning my moves and strategy;
As still in bed I lay.

I had tried suggested methods,
So many times before,
The end result was just the same,
I'd end up on the floor.

As I held my bated breath,
I pushed the corners in,
Starting at the beginning,
The best place to begin.

I eased the cover up carefully;
How I tried and tried,
Both corners kept slipping out again,
'Oh goodness me' I cried,

At last I got the cover on,
'No, no, no!' I began to shout;
As I smoothed the final wrinkle,
I saw the damn thing was inside out.

June Worsell

FRIENDS LIKE THESE

Friends who give
and friends who please -
bless me, Lord,
with friends like these.

Friends who help
and friends who care -
of these friends, Lord,
I ask my share.

Friends who love me
whatever I've done -
these friends, Lord,
are number one.

Happy friends
are such a gift,
and Lord, they help
my spirits lift.

Friends who share
and give their time -
Lord, I'm glad such
friends are mine.

Friends who fill
my life with love -
such friends are gifts
from you above.

Andrea Sandford

THE MADMAN'S RHYME

These fluted shells
Express a subtle will
And airily deny the roughened swell
That cliff-bound wanderers
Shudder to observe.

This purple flower
That blows sweet-scented hours
Belies the wicked hoar
And swingeing hail
Of winter's raillery.

This crystal star
That with such stare
Seeks to outpeer
The awful space of night
Sheds Holy light.

Who can tell how chance and will
Together shape a shell -
A flower or star design?
Or pluck from out the heart
A madman's rhyme?

Terry Smith

YOUR LOT

Along the road from school to home,
The children of the village come,
With pressing haste and eager legs
To buy their chocolate Easter eggs.
Alas, the shop is very small and some
Will get no eggs at all;
And so the first unlucky tot
Must face the answer -

That's shalott.

Janet Cavill

RHYME AND REASON

It's not perverse
To write blank verse,
Quite the reverse!
Be not averse
To scorn the curse
Of matching 'nurse'
Perhaps with 'purse'
Or maybe 'terse' . . .
Yet rhymes diverse
Ne'er make verse worse!

And even Shakespeare found he had the time
To finish off each act with fitting rhyme.

As for metre
Nothing's neater
Than four feet a
Line, or complete a
Brief pentameter
Or three feet more octameter
With tuneful rhymes, sounding sweeter
To every Tom, Dick - and Rita!

A poem with thoughtful rhymes and metred length
Has style, appeal and real poetic strength.

Geoffrey Matthews

THE CONSTANT GUARD

He certainly is not handsome
And would never merit a ransom.
He is barely five feet tall,
His head is too large, his feet too small.
His face is round like the moon,
But the colour of a prune.
He has a mop of tangled hair,
A pop-eyed stare,
A toothless grin
And a receding chin.
His nose is squashed; it's a dreadful sight
And looks as though he has been in a fight.
He wears an old felt hat,
A tattered mac,
Trousers full of holes,
And shoes with flapping soles.
Most people scarcely give him a glance,
Even though he sways as if in a dance.
Children may view his appearance with mirth.
Only the farmer knows his true worth,
As whatever the weather, every day
He stands and scares the crows away.

Dorothy K Springate

ELVES

Eleven elves,
fleet-footed and svelte,
deftly fled the Veld,
and left the twelfth elf,
that slept in felt,
to delve the tilth for Spelt.

Paul Rand

ODE TO MARILYN MONROE

I see you on my calendar, smiling down at me,
I feel your inner beauty that no one could set free.
Your soul was so invaded by tragedy and fame,
That love was never real for you, only fast pace life and gain.

But deep inside your vision, there lay a dream of truth,
You may have died at thirty-six, but you were still a youth.
Sometimes, when I ponder, you speak kind words to me,
And though you lost your pathway, your words are steps I see.

A stairway on to freedom, I'll live the life you lost,
Because my dear friend Marilyn, you haunt me as a ghost.
I sense your spirit gliding, floating through the air,
I see your fluid body; I feel your golden hair.

Marilyn, you still live for me, so deep inside my soul,
That I will live your life again, yes, fulfil all your goals.
So when I see you smiling, I know that I can be,
The living soul that lost is way, and find your destiny.

Sandra Lester

TRAGEDY OF WAR

I sit at peace on this park bench watching children at their play
While dogs of every type and breed chase balls and sticks
their owners throw
and I wonder as I survey this scene about a land so far away
Where a tragedy's unfurled in this land I do not know.

The children they're not in a park, but cowering in a cellar deep
Their parents desperately protecting the ones they love
And the dogs not joyfully chasing sticks upon the lush green grass
But crouched in terror as the bombs rain down from above.

While as the flower of many nations die on the battlefields
Would their dying thoughts question the reason why
In those final seconds when they realise there is no God
And understood why revered leaders are not prepared to die.

Don Woods

SQUARE DEAL

When the love of my life was feeling under par
I booked a *'Square Deal Bargain'* a Thomson two star,
To top up his batteries in a Spanish Shangri-La,
Which is why we are staying at Tossa de Mar.

At the welcome party in our aparthol bar
(Three star rated, with 'happy hour' sangria)
We thought the rep was joking when she smiled and said: 'We are
A good forty minutes walk from Tossa de Mar . . .'
So we coughed up - there and then - to see the silver stars
That pose on the Ramblas outside the tappas bars.
Our Barcelona Highlights has been marvellous (thus far)
Stadium, Church and Snowflake - the zoo's famous star,
And after our picnic - packed in Tossa de Mar,
We will stroll, hand in hand, to see the silver stars,
Posing on the Ramblas outside the tappas bars.

After seven days of sunshine and 'happy hour' sangria,
The love of my life is no longer under par,
Since topping up his batteries in a Spanish Shangri-La,
On our Thompson 'Two star bargain' to Tossa de Mar . . .

Betty Lightfoot

THE QUAY

The breath of the wave rolls onto the sand,
And the fishing boat hugs the sea;
And the moon tears a ragged path through the clouds
As I stand alone on the quay.

But not alone; for there on the boat
Is one who is dear to my heart;
Whose hand on the tiller is steering the boat,
In the fisherman's desperate art.

I watch and watch, and wish that my hand
Were on his to be my guide;
But if that were so, in my heart I know
In his youth he would thrust me aside;

For he loves to sail in the teeth of the storm,
Feel the danger with his own hand;
To steer between the grave at his feet
And the solid rock of the land.

The sea is in murderous mood tonight,
As it tosses the boat to its fate;
And all I can do is stand on the quay
And wait, and wait, and wait.

Julie McAnulty

MY LOVE

I love you for the way you are
to me you're like a shining star
up in the sky where you are free
just watching down upon me

I love the way you make me feel
sometimes I think it's so unreal
to love someone the way I do
and darling that is simply you

To me you are a gift that I
will cherish until the day I die
with you I want to share my life
and hope one day I'll be your wife

When you're in love, then you can say
Oh yeah . . . I felt the same way
It doesn't last for very long
well maybe just for once you're wrong

It's good to find that special one
who's quiet, happy and so fun
he is my soulmate all of the time
without his presence I do pine.

Hyacinth Myers

FEELINGS UPON FEELINGS

Feelings of anger
Feelings of hurt
Feelings of sadness
All make you
Alert

Feelings of guilt
Feelings of remorse
Feelings of grief
We all take
In life's course

Feelings of love
Feelings of lust
Feelings of togetherness
We all can have
When they are
Feelings of
Trust

Maureen Hunter

I BELIEVE IN YOU

You came into my life
Long before I was born,
You made my life and
Created all that I am,
You came into my life
At every port and storm,
And steadied the boat
Which I travelled on.
You led me to safety
Along the path of life,
And encouraged and
Soothed me
In times of strife.
You held my hand
Continually,
And never, ever let go,
What can I say
To thank you -

I believe in You.

Helena Abrahams

BREAK FREE

As evil stalks this earth again,
What chance have we to ease the pain.
The angels seem to have deserted man,
Now all we hear are the pipes of Pan.
The devil offers quick fix cures,
Money and drugs are his lures.
Hatred, greed and avarice rule,
Come one, come all, follow the fool.
Forget to care, ignore earth's need,
Lie, cheat and maim, make this your creed.
The Devil's footprints are deep and clear,
Our demise must make him laugh and cheer.
It's not the thing to believe he's real,
That's how he's got us with his spiel.
'Love conquers all' is out of date,
The evil one has become our fate.
Turn to the light and smile again,
It's kindness that will ease the pain.
Don't judge each other, learn to forgive,
Offer joy and friendship, learn to live.
Smile and be happy. What? So you look a fool,
Just know evil shrivels as you break its rule.
Caress our earth and feed goodness in,
Don't worry at setbacks, just aim to win.
Turn to the light and make it your goal,
Pray to your god to make you whole.
Why bother you say? No one does it for me.
Why not? It's a start to your mind breaking free.

Beth Young

ON WRITING IN RHYME

You have asked me to write
A poem in rhyme
But my mind is a blank -
As it is most of the time!

Of what shall I write?
I haven't a clue.
Mr Kipling I'm not -
But neither are you!

The world is so full
Of a great many things
So what shall I choose -
Cabbages or kings?

Cabbages are green,
Kings are so rare -
I've never met one
But what do I care?

I'm sure what you seek
Is not such a jingle,
But I'll send it in hope
With laughter you'll tingle!

I shall watch in the post
For rejection slip white -
Great poem this ain't,
But it's been fun to write!

Maria-Christina

SOME DAUGHTERS DO 'AVE 'EM

'Mother my romance is over'
Dear daughter has blown it again,
When we met, once or twice
Boris seemed very nice,
And does have a villa in Spain.

Boris is not very handsome,
(Out of ten? A generous two!)
But rich daddy's in oil
Always eager to spoil,
And the penthouse has a good view.

All daughter's chins have been lifted -
At last count, I'm sure she had three;
I despair of her nose
That she foolishly chose,
And didn't inherit from me.

She now needs a sugar daddy
Who's possibly senile but kind;
She may say he's too old
I'd think diamonds and gold,
Small luxuries I wouldn't mind.

Now, silly girl's getting married
This time, cooking oil is to blame,
Cancel private jet trips
Daddy sells fish and chips,
No holiday freebies in Spain.

On hearing my news poor Boris
Sought motherly comfort from me;
He may be short-sighted
But I'm just delighted -
The penthouse is my guarantee!

Doreen Lovey

THE LANGLEYS

They moved into the village back in 1953,
Flats now stand where cows had grazed and houses, like a sea,
Wash over fields that lead to town while any gaps between
Hold small industrial units and a plant for Terylene.

For their shopping and their pensions they have to go to town -
'The heart's gone from the village since the General Store shut down,
We need a butcher and a baker - not a video shop;
It used to be so pretty here, when will the changes stop?'

A mosque gleams on the corner where the Baptist Hall has been;
The language at the bus stop is aggressive and obscene;
'Young kids with their loud music while we're waiting in the queue
And if you're walking to the shops they'll skateboard straight at you.'

'See the turbans in the High Street and dreadlocks on the bus,
And though we feel like strangers here we never make a fuss
Although we can't get tea and cakes because the café's shut -
These days it's all samosas, kebabs or Pizza Hut.'

'The park is not a place to go - it's where the druggies meet,
There's winos in the toilets when it's cold out on the street;
The Market is the only place in town that's stayed unchanged -
The Council plan to close it for a new BT exchange.'

'There's detergent in the fountains and rubbish in the streets -
There's dog mess and old Coke cans when it used to be kept neat -
We'd rather not come into town, but where else can we go?
To see the way the town's gone down - it makes us feel so low.'

They thought this place would see them out, their lives would
                                        be complete:
But village life and countryside have changed - made obsolete
By an all consuming modern world engulfing simple lives -
They're trapped in dark suburbia, just trying to survive.

Patrick Osada

COLOUR BAR, NONE

Imagine a world of black and white
Without a single colour in sight.
With only grey objects to view.
Dark skies that are never blue.

But definitions are still found
Even when monochromes abound . . .
For white, needs the black's meaning
As black does, to white's screening.

It's the print that points the way
And as those written forms display.
But colour creeps into the frame
In memories, that words contain.

Interpretations vary in hue
With the differing points of view.
Perceptions modify the shade
From which each montage is made.

It's diversity of tones
That gives muscles to the bones.
That animates those sepia prints
With the wondrous coloured tints.

And like that brush stroke artistry
Words weave coloured in tapestry,
With their black and white foundations
Bloom those various presentations . . .

For words can resonate
To a colour coded bait;
And print never can be dead
When this black and white is, read!

H D Hensman

DREAMTIME

His hands upon my back, like morning waves upon the beach -
Rolling in.
Fine, tanned and thin, cool and cleansing on my skin.
On my neck and head, fingers spread, lifting gently thro' my hair
From nape to crown, and slowly down.
The smooth inner face of his arm, drifting on my back - slack.
Like smoothest satin slipping by, skims my shoulders, charms my arms,
Then taking sides - slides
Stroking light and lingering on the length of my thigh,
Floating fingers that dip behind the knee,
Following the muscle contour to the heel - tenderly.
Palms along the reaches of my feet, outstretched -
His fingers on my toes, slipping into those.
Tongue touching fingertips and fluttering on my lips.
My muscles loosen, stretch and shed all stress.
Warm feelings in my head, ripples of pure pleasure tease my skin.
I shiver in their wake, concentric ripples on a lake.
Leave me centred on a higher conscious plane -
To face the world again. Such tender touch,
Like sprinkled sand, takes me to another land.

Marilyn Hodgson

A Bright Little Sparky

A little naughtiness, now and again is fine,
Just so long, as we both know
Where to draw the line.

My little dog Sparky, loves to have fun,
Bringing happiness and laughter to almost everyone,
Doing his utmost and very best to amuse,
Driving away all my troubles and blues.

The truth is, I love him,
He's the apple of my eye,
When he is around me,
I would never want to cry.

Long may he live,
My little companion and friend,
Cos I for one, never want us to end.

Susan Barker

U R YY 2B TES

You are too wise to be upset
By messages on phones in text
Loving English grammar but yet
Not willing to be easily vexed

You always say 'different from' not 'to'
Wince when people say 'you know'
At every sentence end. They do.
Or else they say 'I mean'. It's so

Frustrating for a language buff
And yet you smile and listen still
You don't fret if the accent's rough
But note each word, through good and ill

'It's what they need to say that matters'
Is your attitude to other folk
Listen to those with lives in tatters
And cheer them with a little joke

So keep in touch by phone and pen
Do not rant and pontificate
You'll never lose touch with children
So long as they communicate.

John M Spiers

PIPE DREAMS

If I'd the courage and the money
to follow what's in my head
I'd buy myself a camper van
and maybe I'd paint it red.
To travel the roads in freedom
and stop where fancy took me
I'd do nothing but sit
and think, and, oh, just be.
I'm not at all a noisy person
but in the street I'd sing aloud
If it were not for others disapproval
covering free spirit like a cloud.
I'd wear anything at all I liked
not care if I attracted a stare
With others thoughts I'd not bother
it would be entirely my affair.
I have neither the money or courage
so I conform just like a slave
Anyway I'm more than fifty now
so I suppose I must behave.

Kathy Slade

A CURE FOR WRINKLES

My skin was looking wrinkled,
Just like waves upon the sea;
Then the phone rang - made me jump.
The ceiling bashed my knee!

I crawled towards the telephone,
My sore knee made this tryin' . . .
I don't have wrinkles anymore -
Not since I used an iron!

The caller was a friend of mine,
Who told me what to do:
'Don't worry about your wrinkles, chum;
Go to the local zoo.

There is a keeper working there,
And he has trained a lion
To smooth the skins of elephants
By using a warm iron!'

So I set off for the zoo -
Did this thing really work?
If so, I'd try it on myself;
If not, I'd feel a berk!

It worked! It worked! What can I say?
Oh, thanks for phoning, friend!
Although this story isn't true,
It's got a happy end!

Roger Williams

BIRTHDAY TREAT - A TRUE TALE

Mum's in the kitchen
Making jellies in a dish
Tomorrow's party will be the best
A three-year-old could wish.

In comes Simon eager to see
What the birthday treats will be
Reaches up to catch the dish
'Mum, what have you put in this?'

Alas the counter's just too high
For little Simon's questing eye
He tips the dish, the contents pour
All over him and on the floor.

Calling to big sister
To take him up the stair
Mum runs the bath and strips his clothes
Washes jelly from his hair.

His tears soothed and over
Mum stands at the kitchen door
The cat is 'jellied' to the mat
The mat 'jellied' to the floor.

About an hour later
Simon's asleep in bed
Dreaming of his birthday
And the treats he will be fed.

Mum is back in the kitchen
Making jellies in a dish
Tomorrow's party will be the best
A three-year-old could wish.

Joan Gray

MY GARDEN

My garden's in a sunny spot,
Consisting of a flower pot,
That sits upon my window sill,
Precariously poised to kill
Some unsuspecting soul below,
With more than just a glancing blow.

But stay your hand and do not fret,
Pray do not call a policeman yet,
For doubtless you'll be pleased to know,
It's for the Chelsea Flower Show.
My orchid's tethered to the wall,
And guaranteed - yes - not to fall!

Gilbert Russell

TOMORROW

For the school,
a poem for you all.
Think of you writing and thoughts
inside your head.
Think of the way you write, or of
what has been said.
The learning,
the result,
the help, yes the truth.
Learn and be good,
learn and grow up,
think of today
and the whole life to play.
Listen to your teacher,
yes all the way.
Make the best,
don't waste time,
this is a rule
it can be fine.
Don't bully
don't fight,
think of the future,
it can be bright.

Shauna Hamilton

RED ADMIRAL

. . . Such colour of life the admiral led,
So elegant and high,
Till caught out in his flutterings
Did see a flower nearby . . .
Enchanted with this pure delight,
Abandoned for a time, his flight . . .
In grassy bed of shade, so deep
A fold of velvet red undone, so fresh,
As Anastasia sleeps,
Lay soft the hazing, fazing sun
This single rose upon.
Reflecting at her slumbering here
(Which slight did entertain a tear
Within a fluttered eyelid shed
To fall upon this rose so red
All for a love, no longer near) -
The admiral, aroused did flit
This tempting perfumed form toward,
All unawares, enticed abroad . . .
In sunlit flight of fancy soared
And thus in nectar sweet repose
Did light upon his chosen rose,
For two were they *but* chose he one
And hovered o'er her breath anon . . .
In stealing one momentary kiss
Did she awake askance at this . . . !
The admiral was gone.

Roger Mosedale

A Derelict Cottage

A little cottage seated on a hill
Sturdy and strong 'gainst all the wind and rain,
A haven for the heart to nestle in,
Where peace restores the mind and eases pain.

Empty it now stands, aloft, forlorn,
Where once its shelter shielded those within,
Where is the throbbing life that it has known,
The love, the laughter of one's kith and kin?

The walls are weathered now and bleak to view,
Where crumbling stones are starting to fall down,
The windows grimy, growing mosses too,
The roof, like sorrow, covering its brow.

Inside, the doors are dirty, cupboards too,
Where still some pieces of old delph remain,
Clothed in dust, whose coating hides from view,
Speckled ones, and blue, with someone's name.

The kitchen's rusty stove and sink remain,
No longer used and long since left to time,
The curtains still hang on a windowpane,
Thick with years use and dust, and grease and grime.

The stairs are tottering, unsafe to tread,
But looking up, I just can see around
An open door, an old and dingy bed,
And pieces of old clothes upon the ground.

The lounge is empty now and sad to view,
A mouldering carpet lies upon the floor,
Unfurnished now, but in my mind I see,
The loveliness within when it was new.

Bridget Rose Peck

THE TWELVE APOSTLES

The twelve left their homes, their trades and all,
When Jesus the messiah gave them a call.
At his voice they obeyed without any regrets,
Got up and left their boats and their nets.

Most of the twelve were fishers by trade.
Fishers of men by him they were made.
They heard him teaching the crowds day by day.
'He teaches with authority,' they heard them say.

They saw him heal people with all kinds of sickness.
They marvelled to see the cured people bear witness.
He was with his disciples by day and night.
They saw the dead raised and the blind receive sight.

They witnessed his death on the cruel cross,
Full of joy when he rose to restore their loss.
On his mission he sent them, to do just the same:
'Preach, teach and baptise, and heal in my name.'

They suffered for this a severe persecution,
Most of them martyrs through fell execution.
But their mission bore fruit and churches were founded
In Asia and Europe and Christians abounded.

For their lives we heartily thank you, O Lord.
They fulfilled your command and obeyed your word.
These saints are alive and praise you in heaven.
In your service their all they had boldly given.

David Shrisunder

DIFFERENT LOVES

Different kinds of love for different people
Spell out the ways, write it down in words
The love of a child as it suckles your breast
The love of your man, could it be the best

Then the love of woman to woman
No different from many other loves
Unusual, unforeseen, a true test
Yet many say love with a woman
Is the only way to hold a caress.

So whatever your love, it's your own
Just cherish and hold if forever
Never, let yourself be alone
Just be thankful, true love you've been shown.

E Corr

QUIXOTE LIVE AGAIN

To tilt at windmills is absurd, but not to is obscene.
No children born with wasted form, should this not be our dream.
Eat Sunday's lunch and Monday's brunch, your suppers while
                                        you may.
Eat breakfast too and Irish stew, don't give a scrap away.
Then lick your lips at fish and chips and with your fork held high.
Your mind engrossed with beans on toast or steak and kidney pie.
So raise your bowl and drink your soul, and swallow it with pride.
Backfill the hole then purge your soul, ten thousand more just died.
To eat's the game and who can blame a trencherman forsworn,
Who looks at life twixt fork and knife, 'Ten thousand more are born,'
He cries with glee and all can see his swollen gut all paid.
'But on this day I beg to say, ten thousand more are laid.'
Through hunger's pain the rest are slain, but who can tell the score.
Here's to the day when we can all say, 'Quixote rides once more.'
So tilt your lance and take a chance at windmills now and then.
With greed your aim, to fails no shame, 'Quixote, live again!'

B N Greenway

THE TASTY BOY

I know a little boy who has a strawberry nose,
Two fried eggs for eyes, and jam between his toes,
And the girls all think he's tasty, and really quite a dish
With his long spaghetti hairstyle, and breath that smells of fish;

He thinks he looks so cool, as he licks his chocolate fingers,
But since he's had a fizzy drink, there's an awful smell that lingers,
It's hard to know if he's popped, or burped, because it
                                                    was half-hearted,
Then the teacher got a whiff of it, and this is when it started;

He said that he felt really sick, as he staggered towards the door,
And his jelly legs went wobbly as they bent and touched the floor,
His swollen face turned cabbage green, and his lips were all a quiver,
His banana arms waved up and down, he was about to lose his dinner.

As he zig-zagged along the corridor he looked an awful sight,
And heading towards the toilets he squeezed his bottom tight,
But this story I won't finish, I will leave the end to you,
Did he loose his dinner or did he make the loo?

P J Cain

THE BORED DOG

I snap at the flies and chase after bees -
They buzz all around and just make me sneeze.
I bark at the cat but she won't come and play,
She claws at my nose, and then runs away.
I sniff round the grass in search of a mole
But they are so scared they just run down a hole.
We go for a walk, my master and me,
But he won't let me stop when I find a nice tree.
He is such a bore, he keeps throwing me sticks
And when we meet friends he makes me do tricks.
I take him his slippers and sit up and beg,
But really I'd like to get hold of his leg!

J Bryan

SPIDER

Stretched across the window
Hangs a silken spider thread
Arachnid in the centre
Waiting to be fed

Patience is a virtue
Thinks the spider to itself
Until some tasty morsel
Climbs on my larder shelf

When an unsuspecting fly
Lands upon my silver home
I'll unwrap it safe in argent cord
So no more will it roam

And when I'm good and hungry
I'll help myself to food
Delicate and tasty
And so improve my mood.

Tracy Enright

I AM THAT I AM

I am that I am
Nothing can change that.
Expected to please
A desire to tease
Spotless also respectful
Sparkling and helpful

I am that I am
Nothing can change that.
Attentive plus sharing
Hanging thus caring
The truth is, it is just the way I am.

I am that I am
Nothing can change that.
Weedy, weak and shameless
Wicked, sinful and ruthless
Perfect in my imperfection
Losing a little of me.

I am that I am
Nothing can change that.
Clean then quiet
Calm, peaceful, then silence
I am that I am.

Rowland Macaulay

IF WISHES WERE HORSES

If some good fairy came to me
And said, 'One wish - what shall it be?'
I wouldn't need to rack my brain;
I'd say, 'Please turn time back again.'
I'd do the things all left undone
And sing the praises left unsung.
I wouldn't 'wait another day'
I'd deal with all that came my way.
Take back the words best left unsaid,
Read all the books so far unread.
Offers of help I wouldn't spurn,
All friendly smiles I would return.
I'd be a perfect wife and mum,
A friend in need, a 'good old chum'.
But that, of course, can never be:
So I'm just stuck with the real me.
Stumbling along life's stony path
With, now and then, a cheerful laugh,
And hope I'll never lack a friend
To share my troubles 'til the end.

Val Carter

WELCOME TO HELL!

Tears fall as I
    read of the heartaches
And yet a smile
    when their bravado calls -

Tell me now -
    are you so brave
Are you so innocent -
    can you honestly judge
those behind prison bars?

Have you not killed
    in thoughts of vengeance
Choking the light
    so deep down within -

You who are Judas
    and weakling like Pontious,
Betray all the good
    which Lord Jesus did bring.

Mary Skelton

THE FLOWERING

Sarah, Suzanne and Georgina,
Three daughters of highest degree.
Their mother, the fairest Robina,
Their father, the brave Anthony.

Sarah, Suzanne and Georgina,
Three maids in a castle so fine,
Bounded by gardens and fountains,
Where leaves of japonica climb.

Where sun through the panes of the casement,
Sends shafts of bright gold on their heads,
Solemnly bended together,
With secrets and dreams to be shed.

The trees in the garden grow taller,
The flowers their petals spread wide,
But Sarah, Suzanne and Georgina,
Are flowers that are growing inside.

The castle walls guard them in childhood,
The chains of love hold them all fast,
But the soft, silken rope of their binding,
Will gentlier break at the last.

And out of the castle they'll wander,
Dancing their way through the years,
And the brave Anthony and Robina,
Will silently banish their tears.

Barbara J Settle

DREAMING OF LEMONS

I have a baby lemon tree
now nearly six months old.
Slowly a tiny pip has grown
I've watched each leaf unfold.

Branches are forming on it now -
first one, then two, then three.
When will I have a yellow fruit
upon my lemon tree?

Will you come when the fruits are ripe?
I'll make a marinade
to tenderise your chosen steak;
while sipping lemonade.

We'll share the luscious yellow fruits.
So come and visit me.
It is my dream that I will pick
fruits from my lemon tree.

Evelyn Golding

RENEWED POWER

Tongues that freeze
The apple of the eye
As one sees
But bear no sigh
Looking upward
There abounds
A kind of reward
For thy head to crown

Such days will occur
Thy destiny to destroy
But can be a sign to onward spur
Filling one with glory
For a while feelings hurt
But seek thee peace
Making thee alert
And problems to cease

When so burdened
Lift up thy eyes
Converse with a friend
To banish thy sighs
One then feels
Fresh as a flower
Nodding in the breeze
Filled with renewed power.

Josephine Foreman

BUSTER

My sister June in hospital (a sorry sight to see),
Was victim to an incident of great intensity.
It happened on a Thursday and few knew of her plight,
Whose thoughts were of her puppy dog whom she had left that night.
T'was during late hours Friday, at eight o'clock spot on,
A friendly voice phoned plaintively to say June's dog had gone,
To neighbours living in the street, (across the way I hear),
Stating that the dog was ill and would I lend an ear?
To, complaints ranging from its health, to what I aim to do,
Since this poor pup, it wasn't theirs, (t'was really up to you)
Therefore I rang the local vet who clearly had his say,
'Just bring him in for ten o'clock, tomorrow, Saturday.'

But, nine o'clock the pup was dead and 'Bill' old chap was lost,
He couldn't put that dead dog out that night at any cost.
Bang on nine that self same night my contact phoned to say,
'This pup that's dead, what shall we do? Can you take it away?'
'Of course I said - But not tonight' - (T'was raining heavens hard!)
'Tomorrow morn at ten o'clock, please put it in the yard.'
But Bill old chap, emotional, replied, 'I'll wrap it up!'
'When you collect, please promise me, find out what killed that pup!'
I fetched it on the Saturday and took it to the plot,
Then buried 'Buster' 'neath the soil, its mortal form to rot.
I later asked a female 'cop' 'Procedure, if you please,'
'Should this recur some future date, do I bury 'neath the trees?'
Quote she, 'The local dustcart will dispose of without doubt.'
I thought of 'Bill',
      Then June and I,
            That dog dug in,
                  Said nowt.
The moral of this story is, this problem when you're dead,
Few people know just what to do, and why few tears are shed.
And living seems no different when so many fail to care,
For those of us surviving this old age and wear and tear.

D Turberfield

THE QUIET LIFE

They say we climb a mountain
Just because it's there
I don't want to climb a mountain
I prefer my own armchair
Some of us have journeyed
To lands both near and far
Some have even reached the moon
For me that's much too far
There are men with lots of courage
Who will always do or die
Men who seek for hidden truths
In the ocean and the sky
Not for me the glory
The praises and acclaim
For daring deeds of courage
The accolade of fame
Let others seek adventure
I know I'd never dare
I prefer the quiet life
With time to stand and stare.

Lydia Barnett

CATCH ME A MUSE

Thoughts never come in numerous herds
They sneak around all solitary
Striving to find those erudite words
To make eye-catching verses that vary

How would it feel if I happened to win?
A wordly competition for poets
How can I successfully spin?
To best all those clever know it's

A lack of my language does naught to help
While this is the ultimate test
Pregnant brain needing a push to whelp
Thoughts aimed at making mine best

Lack of words may make me rue it
Someday maybe I will get to learn
Just how famous authors do it?
While we talentless amateurs just 'burn'

It's the huffing and puffing that divides
The grown-ups from the kids
Like trying some clever and witty asides
To further our literary bids

Never being much in the way of a swot
And an early school leaver
Thirty lines seems to be quite a lot
To this erstwhile eager beaver

It has so often been truly said
Quit while in the lead
And if you have managed to get ahead
Never rue the deed.

John Of Croxley

CRIES FROM THE HEART

Look, look into our eyes
    and see the sorrow there.
Look into our hearts and see the longing.
Look into our minds
    and see the thoughts of despair.
Listen to the songs in the air.

Understand the message
    that is sent on the wind.
Comprehend the grief and the sorrow.
Understand the anguish
    of a nation at war
and realise we have no tomorrow.

Keep our starving families
    from death, one more day.
Keep us safely housed from the cold.
Give us just enough
    to keep our babies alive
and tell us what we have to be told.

That we are the innocent,
    we are the poor.
We are the ones you will save.
Unless we are caught
    in the fight for our lives
then we'll be the ones for the grave.

Sylvia Shepherd

RHYMING CHALLENGE

R isking rejection
H ating selection
Y ou submit your rhyme.
M etre is perfect
I mages reflect
N uances abound.
G enerally sound.

C ounting off each day.
H oping come what may.
A t last your reply.
L onging for support,
L ocating report
E agerly waiting
N erve endings grating.
G o on, take a look!
E ntered in their book?

Catherine Craft

RHYMING SLANG

Beautifully blonde, her Barnet Fair,
Long and shiny, was her hair.
Looking radiant in her tit-for-tat,
Like a queen wearing, an Ascot hat.

Shining brightly were, those pork pies,
Long lashes surrounding, dark brown eyes.
Silence, broken by the dog and bone,
Came a shrill ring from the phone.

Aching and hot plates of meat,
So sore and red, those poor feet.
Feeling more than, a little cream crackered,
Never before felt, quite so knackered.

She's arrived now, our Rosie Lea,
Time to sit and enjoy, a cup of tea.
Hoping that I, at last have the hang,
Of writing this poem, in rhyming slang.

June F Allum

POETIC LABOURS

One day I thought I'd have a bash
At writing verse like Ogden Nash;
The outcome was so awfully thin
I threw my efforts in the bin.

I tried to write, next, like Pam Ayres,
But boredom caught me unawares;
I doodled up to ten o'clock
Then went to bed with writer's block.

Alas, I'd never have a hope
To write like Alexander Pope,
Or scale the heights of Keats or Shelley -
I'll chuck it in and watch the telly!

Anthony Manville

OH! WHAT A PITY

Oh! What a pity we had not thought,
Of the importance of what Granny taught,
That sex before marriage was extraordinarily fraught.

Young people we know want to enjoy,
A special togetherness with immediate joy,
This applies it seems to both, the girl and the boy,

But when it goes beyond the joy and the fun,
The oven is often filled with a currantless bun,
Followed quite often with the boy on the run,
And followed by the girl's father with a 'bloody big' gun!

All this brings misery, often called grief,
And the boy is branded a cad and a thief,
And the girl is stuck with the results, of a short-term relief.

Leslie Loader

RHYMING CHALLENGE

'A' comes before 'B', 'B' comes before 'C'.
Like this present for me at 'Christmas',
As the wind juggled my boat on the *pond*
Now, how back to me will it *respond*?

I ran to the other side of the *pond*,
For surely it must land *here*,
But a shift in the wind sent it *careering*
Nearly upside down. Quick! What comes after 'C'.

'Ahoi' I cried, to the imaginary crew
And thought I heard an answering shout.
Was it a pirate ship, for me, they had *chose*
But I was still stuck on 'C', hiding *below*.

Suddenly a car on the shore back 'fired'
'That's more like it,' I shouted to the wind,
As he blew my toy boat close to me in 'fun'
And I looked around me for a toy 'gun'.

I found a long length of 'hardwood'
And aimed it at my toy boat.
I hadn't noticed the storm coming up
And the crash of thunder made me 'jump'.

The lightning flashed, the thunder *clashed*,
I had my toy boat to the pier *lashed*,
It was so small and the masts so high
The waves toppled it over, easy as *pie*.

I was so moved by the sinking of my toy
I held a ceremony for all to enjoy.
'A', 'B' and 'C' headed the procession
And 'X', 'Y' and 'Zee' finished the challenge.

Rosemary Smith

DAY TRIPPER TO SEASIDE

Standing on the shore, looking out to sea.
At ships on the horizon. In total there was three.
Then to my amazement, I looked along the sand;
And there I saw two people, walking hand-in-hand.

They went behind a rock, and laid upon the ground.
And in the gentle breeze, I heard a funny sound.
I wondered what it was, and went to have a look.
And all that I could see; was them two, and a duck.

The tide was rolling in, the waves were four feet high.
With deckchairs on the sand, and seagulls in the sky.
I looked the other way, and saw a little boat.
Bobbin' up and down, trying to get afloat.

The promenade was heaving, with people having fun.
Holding their ice cream, melting in the sun.
With bingo numbers calling, from the penny arcade.
As some little children, drank their lemonade.

The air was quite embracing, I felt a little chill.
But I was at the seaside, and it was such a thrill.
I don't have many pleasures, and I don't make much fuss.
But when I looked around, I missed the bloody bus.

If this is Sunday outings, I'm going to stop at home
And potter in my garden, tending to the loam.
At least it isn't raining, that's something to be thankful for.
Or I'd have been pissed off! Stood here on this shore.

When I see the beggars, that left me stranded here.
I'll tell them what I think; and what to do next year.
If only they had waited, instead of pissing off.
I'd have been as happy, as pigs swill in a trough.

Martin Snowdon

NOTHING ON TV

There's nothing on the TV
Why am I so bored?
The meal's in the microwave,
The TV dinner's thawed.
If there's something worth watching
Then my logic's flawed.
Sex and violence tends to pall.
Like a diet of chips,
It'll do you no good at all.

Drowning in a sea of moral pollution,
Give three cheers to the broadcasting revolution.
Pornography is simply not the solution.
I've had all the quiz shoes I can take,
And a bunch of chancers on the make.
I don't care about being a millionaire,
All I want is a world that's fair.
And another real-life documentary
Will drive me crazy,
Just entertainment for the terminally lazy.
And voyeurs watching poseurs,
Soon to be festooned with digital delights,
Watching garbage late into the night.
It wants to make you take flight
From a world gone mad.
Television really is that bad.

N A Wilford

On The Move

Hmm . . . I think Mum says we call this a wire,
But why's it stuck in this thing, called a fire?
Blowed if I know, but it needs a good tug,
Oops . . . too hard, fallen back on the rug.

Wow! This is great! They call this the bin,
Well almost managed to squeeze myself in,
But why's all this stuff in here anyway?
Best take it out, and make room to play.

Oh what a struggle, I'm worn-out, phew!
Heard Mum and Dad say, this is the loo,
I'll just drop this in, and this thing as well,
'Don't do that!' she's starting to yell.

Now let me see, this looks really good,
She tells everyone, 'It's all solid wood',
Ouch! That hurt, Mum says it's a bump,
Then makes it cold, and calls it a lump.

Can't catch this thing, keeps running away,
Perhaps that's why they keep telling it . . . stay!
Don't seem to like me, pulling its hairs,
Spends lots of time, under the stairs.

What is this? Ugh! Food it ain't!
I think Dad said, we call this paint,
I've seen him splashing it on the door,
So I'll just tip it out, all over the floor.

Mum tells me, we call this stuff food,
And don't play with it, cos that's kinda rude,
Says, 'Don't you splatter it up the wall!'
Tut . . . Well can't I have any fun at all!

Allison Dawn Fowles

TOPSY LOU-LOU JANE

The light of my life has left me,
My little one's gone away.
But she'll live in my heart forever,
And we'll be back together one day.
Her black shiny coat will be glistening,
Her green-golden eyes I will see,
And she'll purr the warm purr of contentment,
Just my Topsy Lou-Lou and me.
Till then I'll remember the good times,
When she was close by my side,
My dear little pussy-cat daughter,
In my heart she'll always abide.
And I know when the Lord comes to call me,
To His heavenly garden above,
My Topsy's waiting there for me,
With her naughty mischievous love.
And as we walk in His beautiful garden,
My pussy-cat Jane and me,
We know we'll never be parted,
Close together we always will be.

Pat Weeks Goodridge

THE OLD CONCERT PIANIST

He listened to the music he'd recorded long ago,
His slippers tapping gently in the firelight's eerie glow;
Arthritic hands betrayed him - he could no longer play -
Now he listened to his music from far off yesterday.

His right hand held a dagger with a sharp and pointed blade
As he listened to the music his now withered soul had made.
His laden heart remembered each and every key,
And all the accolades and praise there always used to be.

Now his spirit soared aloft again as silently he heard
The music speaking to him, each silver note a word.
He listened with attention, to every passing note:-
He listened to his music -
    then simply cut his throat . . .

Anne Rolfe-Brooker

SUCH AS THIS

Upon a windswept path I trod a
tarmac lawn of sprouting weeds,
a single flower, a seeded pod,
had grown defiant, amongst
the dead decaying leaves,
then raised its head, to tempt,
the pale retreating sun,
surely nature could not dismiss
and leave her work undone,
even in a garden such as this.

Edna M Sarsfield

SMOKE!

I gotta have a fag, oh please do let me smoke
I know it's a bad habit, you think that it's a joke
I only have eight a year
That won't hurt me much my dear
Oh let me have a fag.

Oh just a little ciggie you know that it won't hurt
You're really being very mean and rubbing in the dirt
I need to have a little puff every now and then
I've got no other vices - no drinking and no men
Oh let me have a fag.

I gotta have a cigarette, oh do you have a light?
I've sat and sewn up swimming bags for nearly half the night
I won't smoke in your presence, I'll stroll around the pond
And know that it's a smelly habit and that you're not all fond
Oh let me have a fag.

Oh let me have some nicotine, I gotta have a fix
I know we all do funny things to go and get our kicks
I don't mind a roll-up, I've got my Rizzla Red
I'll go and have a smoke out there in the garden shed
I gotta have a drag!

Val Hoare

FIEND-O-FELLOW

Beware, no *be aware*
Why? Why I hear you say
because you can never be too careful;
at this time of day

Why? What time is upon my watch?
I shudder to think if you got lost
Asking the time and walking in places
talking to strangers with peculiar faces
Coming here pretending to want answers
well let me tell you what your chance is
Chances of getting away, away from here
I'd balance the scale of your growing fear
that you'd be scared out of your wits end
by the time I've finished talking to you my friend

Well, let's see, you're walking down a deserted street
unexpectedly you meet
a fellow, a good-looking chap
with a nice woolly jumper and a fashionable looking hat
And he tells you that he has lost a valuable thing
you ponder to think and stand wondering
'This poor young man desperate and sad to have misplaced
his belongings, to be searching in haste'
You offer to help but the fellow declines
insisting that quite soon he would find
And so you go about your way
But in shock you discover that what you thought was day
has suddenly turned to the dead of night
You turn to ask the fellow near only then to discover he has disappeared
Accumulating fear takes its toll but you force yourself to be bold
to go on home, to find your way
hoping that the light of day
would gather soon that you'd be safe in your room,
in your bed to rest your merry, tired, little head.

So walk you do and talk you don't, for there's no one to see
to say hello or smile to happily
And then suddenly *boo!*
Who is standing before you?
Why, it's that good-looking fellow who had lost his belongings
Only now he doesn't look too friendly or too lost
In fact he seems quite hungry and very engrossed
'D-d-did you find what you were looking for?' you cry
'Oh yes, indeed I did,' was the reply
And without haste he grins to reveal,
some rather large fangs of sensitive feel
'I feel very contented for I've found my appetite'
And with that he gives you a great, deep *bite!*

Well there you go, a sorry end
for a helpless, misguided friend
But stay if you may, I suddenly feel peckish
Quite fancy a raw blood and meat dish?

Mary Ibeh

AN IDEALIST WORLD

Imagine a world without war and bloodshed
where people are killed and just left for dead
imagine a world without hunger and poverty
where people starve and live without property

but instead imagine this
where life could be bliss
where people world-wide speak with honesty
no two-facedness and sincerity
where words are sufficient, no need for war
so more wealth in funds to help the poor
and world-wide starvation and poverty no longer exist
people living as brothers and sisters and who insist
that nobody ever live alone.

Patricia A Taylor

MOVERS AND SHAKERS

Eureka! A house to meet your dreams
Now you are bursting at the seams
Elin, Bethan and little James
Need more space for fun and games

The agent arrives all in a flurry
And knows that you are in a hurry
'24 hours is all we'll need
And you'll be on your way at speed.'

The viewers arrive in quite a state
Hot and bothered if they are late
They really are a breed apart
You sense that from the very start.

Soon into every room they roam
And always treat it as their home
They tap the walls and bang the floors
Open cupboards and shake the doors.

Off outside they wend their way
Ever ready to have their say
'Does your garden face east or west?
At the end of the day the south is best.'

'We're sold you know,' they say with glee
'But oh so many more to see.'
They may or may not be in touch
Although they like yours very much.

Then on the horizon you spot a buyer
Your spirits now could not be higher
So happily you'll be home and dry
And wave your shakers a fond goodbye.

Tessa Dewhurst

THE VERSE GETS WORSE AND WORSE

So we are challenged to write in rhyme:
I cannot resist this at any time
whether it's serious or pantomime
provided I don't have to keep it up.

Well, it's back to work though I'm past my prime
and young folk think it's an awful crime
to dig about in the muck and slime
just to make your efforts look like poems.

I'm running out of rhyming runes,
I've played out all the old, old tunes
falling back on moons and spoons
but I've got nowhere really.

Of could I could try pararhymes
and roll off poems in reams and reams
until I'm bursting at the seams
but that may be cheating a bit I think.

My rhymes will show such radiance
as to blind my massive audience
of three; my wife and me and my dog Pence
who's lying at my feet at the moment.

Well, there you are it's all done now
I've struggled through, I don't know how.
I'll stand up now and take a bow
in honour of my stunning verse.

'Bow-wow' sit down, it's awful stuff.
Stop it now, that's quite enough.'
Rhymes indeed, they're crude and rough!

He's not the best judge you know, old Pence.

Norman Meadows

OUR EARTH

If only we could enjoy the world for what it really is,
a beautiful planet, a joy to live on it and treasures to receive,
and if we could only take of it what we really need
But no we don't, so now the warnings all of us must heed.
The grass and trees were oh so green, trees reaching to the sky
but now the trees are falling and the people asking why,
the people who are caring the ones like you and I.
The birds will not be singing in the trees up in the sky
for their habitat is going and they will surely die.
The animals who roamed this place before the human kind
will soon die out and disappear, never to be found.
We must not let this happen, the ones with good intent
this planet isn't ours to kill. it's only ours to rent,
so before there is no turning back we must all look and see
what it is we are doing wrong and we must all agree
that pulling all together and putting things to rights
isn't all that hard you know, we've all fought tougher fights.
So please don't let this world of ours die before our eyes
let's give ourselves this one last chance and really win the prize.

S Seed

THE TRAVELLER

A wanderer in search of sweetest love,
she walks the cobbled stones of life.
Travelling to reach an ordained destiny,
to become a mother, and a wife.

Along the way there are affairs,
with strangers who soon become friends.
She knows these encounters are short-lived,
and sorrow never marks their ends.

Her heart is strong, and survives,
to battle on another day.
While those who she leaves behind,
realise the price their souls must pay.

The force that drives her spirit onwards,
dwells inside of you and me.
Waiting for that one special moment,
when love arrives to set it free.

M A Challis

TARGET PRACTICE

A tranquil scene of meadows green with grass,
A placid herd of cows and playful calves,
But then along come men with noisy tractors
But louder still their guns and cruel laughs.

The cows who graze and suckle tiny offspring
Were slaughtered where they stood with one old bull,
The youngsters used, from what the papers told us,
As target practice in the general cull.

The calves, alone with dead cows all around them,
Then run in panic round and round the mead.
For three long hours their persecutors hunt them
Before they finalise this bestial deed.

At last this dreadful cull is over
And little corpses lie around - some bleed -
Will God forgive the way we treat our livestock
Or pardon those who fouled an English field?

Elizabeth Zettl

SURPRISINGLY ENOUGH

Surprisingly enough
As we live day by day
And we go along gladly
On life's rocky way
We need just a little
A positive thought
Where feelings and sharing
All this can't be bought
Hold on to your faith
It's enlightening true
And you know it can comfort
Will carry you through
A few peaceful moments
Of sweet contemplation
With friends you are fond of
Your closer relations
Spread love then whenever
The need does arise
I think we need faith
It's what keeps us alive
Uplifting your spirit
Whenever you choose
Have faith and believe me
In life you can't lose.

Jeanette Gaffney

WHAT WONDER

I wonder where the sun goes to
when slow it sinks and darkness falls
but then again I wonder too
where hides the moon when daylight calls.
I wonder where the rainbow ends
it never seems to land near me
I see the arch, observe its bend
but where then can its ending be?
I wonder where the rain comes from
it's said it falls from in a cloud
but I was in an aeroplane
above the clouds and rain still round.
I wonder where the water goes
when from a million baths it flows
it's said it's in a reservoir
but surely that would overflow?
I wonder if the stars are there
in daylight but we just can't see
their glow though even in a storm
they're not seen in the gloom above me.
I wonder where the plants all go
when nothing's seen in deep snow's fall
but in the spring they're back again
as the season seems them to call.
I wonder why, I wonder so
yet get no answers though I ponder
ah yes I realise now I'm writing
it's the miracle of nature's wonder.

Channon Cornwallis

THE SPIDER

Oh have you seen a spider's web
On this autumnal morn?
A dew bespangled masterpiece
Shines with the sun at dawn.

Though spiders may arouse your fears,
In nature play their part.
Admire him as he sits enthroned
In all his work of art.

Valerie Small

A Song Thrush Returns

I listened for your voice long years in vain,
Statistics demonstrate a sad decline.
Then unbelievably, the sound I fain
Would hear: and there, outlined
Against the pearls
Of morning you cling in the ash, and skirls

Of thrice repeated song flood waking day.
Unforgettable music of the wild
Triumphant over hurried urban ways,
Thrilling the schoolbound child,
Imperative
Demand to pause, to listen now, to live

Harmoniously with the lesser ones
Who share this earth, which from the chill of space
Men named a jewel; enmeshed in aeons
Uncountable, its face
Alone smiled, breathed,
Flowing with water and light, life bequeathed.

Elinor Wilson

IN AWE

It's there beside you, far away,
In ever, a calling apart,
Does come with, as always,
Though ever so near,
When you whisper, in high note,
An all over sphere,
Where besides, I'm left alone,
To ever, but call out, appear,
I'm left without my new-born day,
That ever describes a night-time away,
The dawn of appearance,
Is there with us still,
In calling its shadows, across yonder hill,
Ere creeping in moment, each second come near,
Is blossomed in rapture
The right time, so clear,
Sunbeam rays across the sky,
Are intermingled and come nearby,
They stretch in awe, the clouds on high,
Outreach, but from a lasting bye,
So but seems it's far away,
Across the dewdrops, more each day,
They in turn give us the whisper,
That comes, but now in play.

Hugh Campbell

I HOPE YOU ENJOYED HOME-GROWN DINNER

I hope you enjoyed home-grown dinner.
Was the 'Franklim' soup purest delight?
'Avoncrisp' or 'Dandie'?
'Ailsa Craig' or 'Pixie'?
'Scarlet Globe' and 'Mantanghong' - just right.

Did you dine on the essence of 'Durham'
Or do you think it stemmed from 'Savoy'?
Was it 'Peer Gynt' you munched on
Or 'Roger' you crunched on?
I'll stand down-wind to fully enjoy!

I hope you enjoyed home-grown dinner
With 'Wilja' and 'White Gem' to eat,
'Cavalier', 'Jubilee'
And 'Rondo' did I see?
Was that 'Lizzy' you had as a treat?

And what did you have for afters?
'Red Lake' or 'Ben Sarek' instead?
Did too much 'White Versailles'
Bring the tear to your eye
Or was it just something I said?

I hope you enjoyed home-grown dinner.
I think you're looking just fine.
I hope you enjoyed home-grown dinner.
(burp) Pardon.
I enjoyed mine.

Lynn M Cochrane

IN MY DREAMS

In my dreams I see you,
Hold you, touch you, feel you.
Yet in my waking hours you're gone
And I'm again, once more alone.

In my dreams you're always there,
I know you love me, know you care.
I hate to wake, once more to see,
You've once again deserted me.

In my dreams I see your face,
And all my hopes fall into place.
But now my eyes are open wide,
You're no longer here, at my side.

In my dreams I'm haunted.
Yet never am I daunted,
I'll search for you when I'm awake,
I'll find you too, make no mistake.

In my dreams, I'm happy and glad,
I love you, so how could I possibly be sad?
So why do I wake in anger and doubt
And watch as my dream just fizzles out?

Trisha Walton

LOVE UNSHARED

Did you love me long ago,
When time was on our side?
Did you want to tell me so,
But couldn't for your pride?
Do the days seem lonely,
The days we never share?
Was I meant to love you only,
Did you ever care?
Was it just my mind,
Playing tricks on me?
What answers would I find,
If our minds could be free?
If words were never spoken,
What treasures in life missed,
Will lonely hearts be broken,
If never loved or kissed?

Geoffrey Woodhead

MOVING ON

This emptiness and stillness, I never thought I'd see,
A shell, it's just a carcass, that's all that's left of me.
The memories of joy, I hear echoing all around,
Each room had life, had meaning, its individual sound.
It's only just a building, should I really care?
I need to stay here longer if just to stand and stare.

Unexpected tears of sadness swell, as I try to blink my eyes,
I feel I'm in turmoil, like the whirlwind of the skies.
My home was so inviting, happiness is always felt so near,
I'm standing in the very place, where comfort once stood here.
It's only just a building should I really care?
I still need to stay here longer if just to stand and stare.

I glimpse outside the window, as my world is upside down,
Children are just playing, don't they know I'm leaving town?
Their loving smiles of freedom in their fearless time of play,
I wish I had that time again, perhaps I will some day.
It's only just a building should I really care?
I will stay a little longer, why does life seem so unfair?

My heart, my soul, my spirit, is no longer in this place,
The walls, the floor, the rooms, the doors are just an open space.
An empty canvas waiting for the artist to perform,
A picture that brings happiness that makes a home feel warm.
It's only just a building should I really care?
I need to stay here longer, as good memories are so rare.

The time's now come I'm moving on, to pastures ever new,
I finally feel excitement after all that I've been through.
I stand and stare upon the path and close the door behind,
With one deep breath I walk away, a smile I suddenly find.
Family, love and happiness are what makes a house a home,
All these I'm taking with me so I'll never be alone.

Karen Prinsep-Moores

GOLF

Golf is an obsession from dawn through the day till night
With Birdies, Bears and Eagles I'm sure that can't be right
I thought it was a game they played with balls and tees and clubs
Come New Year the bills arrive and everyone must pay their subs.

'Fore!' they shout or was it five,
The green's quite clear, but man alive
There are people everywhere it seems,
I can't see them; they must be in my dreams.
'We'll play straight through and let you stay.'
That is what the professionals will say
These amateurs they are just a hoot,
They don't really know how to shoot.

They hit the ball straight down the course,
It rolls over and onwards like a mouse.
'Drinks all round' is the shout,
As they enter the bar in the great club house.
He got a hole in one and that is an occasion,
He's never been more full of elation.
Drinks for his friends and strangers alike,
A shot like that had never seen the light.

There they are at the nineteenth hole,
They have aimed for the flags and pulled the poles
But it's dark now and time to retire,
Time to reminisce around a roaring log fire.
They have had a tiring day walking round the course,
Hitting a ball and discussing of course
The day they retire and what they will do,
After all it's only a hobby.
Do you believe it too?

Sheila M Storr

DRIFTER

Silvery hair tied back with string
Wondering what the day will bring.
Drifting along she lost her way
So many things have gone astray.
Familiar people passing by
Never look her in the eye
Things were different in far-off days
People were happy and caring
In their little ways.
Now other things take pride of place
So tears like rain run down her face.

Lovely skies not always blue
Barriers sometimes obstruct the view
Husband taken in crazy war
Did authority realise the score?
Not one person gives a helping hand
People today just don't understand
As night-time calls nowhere to stay
Not knowing if she'll see another day.
This humble beggar she feels no pain
Sleeping rough in the pouring rain.

Charles B Warcup

CHRISTMAS HORRORS

Christmas Eve
'It's Christmas again and all *that,*'
Said the dog to his buddy, the cat.
'And those kids will arrive,
With new toys, yes all five
And that boy is a right little brat.'

The cat then replied to her friend,
'They'll be driving me quite round the bend.
They'll be pulling my tail,
That I know without fail.
How I long for this Christmas to end.'

Christmas Day
(Cat)   'They've stolen my place by the fire.
             They don't care if I live or expire.'
(Dog)   'But just think of the food,
             That should brighten our mood.'
(Cat)   'But that singing - they're hardly a choir!'
(Dog)   'We'll just have to stick it all out.
             If they tease you, just give them a clout
             With your velveteen paws
             And your sharp little claws,
             That should stop them, without any doubt.'

New Year's Eve
(Cat)   'All's over again till next year,
             When 'the darlings' again will appear,
             So I'll purr and I'll smile.'
(Dog)   'And I'll doze for a while
             And forget all about *Christmas cheer.*'

Nancie Cator

THE MYSTERIOUS STRANGER

Three brothers braved a lake on home-made craft.
The wind grew strong and darkness came about.
A sudden gust then lifted from the raft
The youngest lad - he fell with ne'er a shout.
His brothers tried in vain the boy to save,
He slipped away and sank to murky deep.
A boy of eight, he'd met his early grave
And naught the pair could do, save wail and weep.
With heavy hearts they made towards the shore,
Forlorn and full of grief, bereft of hope
And then, through tear-stained eyes, so red and sore,
A shape they spied on yonder grassy slope.
Their brother, cold and wet, yet safe and well
And what an awesome tale he had to tell.

'I surely would be dead but for a man
And where he came from, this he didn't say.
With hair as white as snow and pale face drawn,
He looked to be a hundred, if a day.
He raised me from that dark and dismal gloom
And carried me to where you find me here,
Then vanished just as quickly as he'd come,
'Twas over in an instant - this I swear.
He said, 'This night, my fate is not for you.'
He knew my fear and bid me not to panic.
His uniform was of the navy blue
And on his coat was - *RMS Titanic.*'

Had this old salt survived that poor ship's plight,
Or was he one that died that fateful night?

Alf Nicholles

DEFINITION

Today the egg-heads seem to say
That rhyming verse is quite passé.
It must be trendy or bizarre,
Must never scan, to get so far
As being printed; but to me
The greatest joy of poetry
Is that it rhymes, is not verbose,
For otherwise it's just bad prose.

Evelyn Westwood

SCHOOLDAYS

I started school when I was four
Never, liked it one bit,
One teacher taught us everything
All day we seemed to sit,
At our desks, dare not move
Or even speak a word,
I often look back in time
It was quite absurd.

I can remember often
My pencil in left hand,
Teacher severely scolded me
In right hand she'd demand,
If I disobeyed her
As sometimes I forgot,
Smack on the hand with a ruler
That was our lot.

I am now ambidextrous
In an awkward sort of way,
Thanks to my dreadful teacher
Called, schooling in my day,
No pleasant memories have I
So why do they all say?
Schooldays are the happiest
Not for me anyway.

J Naylor

MISTY MORNING DIAMONDS

On a misty, autumn morning
As the dewy day is dawning,
Spiders' webs to hedges cling
Just like diamonds sparkling.

On the garden gate and trellis tall,
On the plants that grow beside the wall,
Diamonds which the spiders spun
Glisten in the morning sun.

Diamonds, precious are and rare,
But sparkling webs we all can share,
Though only in the morning sun
For they are gone when morning's done.

Jennet Cook

BAGGAGE

I've never had a hero.
I've never been a fan.
I've never had too much respect
For any single man.

I've never wanted followers.
Not followed any trend.
I've never been a groupie
Nor had too good a friend.

I always travel lightly
To keep my movements free.
The clutter of possessions
Hinders my humanity.

But in all my travels
It's always seemed to me.
The heaviest of baggage
Are not friends, but family.

Harry Lyons

SHADOWS

Why do I chase them day by day,
Dreaming precious hours away?
Why do I reach for stars on high,
Why do I reach and fail, and sigh?

If I could think on concrete things,
And could fly on material wings;
If I could harden my own heart
'gainst the woes and pains that are part
Of the life around me moving,
Toughen my voice, till now soothing,
When a friend begs comfort in need
Or a foe needs some kindly deed.

If I could concentrate on wealth
And giving not a fig for health,
Spend weary hours with dreary books.
Well success comes to him who looks
But this success, so dearly bought,
Is an honour I set at nought,
For I have lakes and woods and streams
And I have hopes and I have dreams.

Why do I chase them day by day,
Shadows dancing sweet life away?
I know not, but should we worry?
A lifetime goes in rather a hurry.

A R Barnes

PART-TIME

It used to be asserted
  And events perhaps confirm it
That we'd each a guardian angel,
  If that is what you term it.

And everyone appointed
  As a baby reached this earth
Was thereupon responsible
  From the moment of its birth.

He had to keep a daily watch,
  A truthful record too,
Of ups and downs and accidents
  And all one strives to do.

A sentimental picture,
  Victorian, I think,
Shows children by their angel saved
  At a precipice's brink . . .

If I've had a guardian angel
  Through all these many years,
I hope he will excuse me
  If I say that it appears
He's not entirely skilful,
  However well he means,
But lets tiresome things befall me
  Before he intervenes.

I'm forced to this conclusion
  Since I heard the ceiling fall;
He's part-time guardian angel, but
  Better than none at all.

Kathleen M Hatton

BROUGHAM CASTLE

Yon castle at Brougham is a lovely sight
When it's all lit up by the moonlight.
Its ruined walls are plain to see
How troubled it was through history.

Through the window high up in the keep
The moon made shadows dance and leap;
From a full moon high in the sky -
If I'd seen a ghost I would have died.

A slight whistling sound I heard
It must have been the wind or a bird.
My mind was really playing tricks,
So I headed for home double quick.

Leaving the castle an owl gave a call
Which didn't help me very much at all.
After crossing the bridge on my way home
Saying I'll never come back here alone.

When I got home I said to my wife
That old castle gave me a fright.
Put on the kettle dear for a cup of tea.
Next time I go will you come with me?

Francis Allen

A SECRET NEVER TO BE TOLD

I'm losing sense of value, of direction, sometimes taste
I won't let the grass grow under my feet, not letting minutes waste
In the wink of an eye or a meeting quite by chance
Go with your head and not with your heart or you'll be led a
merry dance.

Does this person feel the same as you, you often wonder why
You could always ask for yourself, if you weren't so shy
Life is often so demanding and lived at such a pace
If life was a little slower, then all the problems I could face.

Will the letter ever get posted? Will I see it lying on the mat?
Catch a brief moment tomorrow for a cuppa and a chat
Just to catch a glimpse of you, no matter how fleeting
Will put butterflies in your stomach at the next meeting.

Secret - can you keep a secret, lock it away never to be told
A secret between two people that is theirs and theirs to hold
Everyone else suspects but alas without conclusive evidence
A field always looks bigger when you're sitting on the fence.

L Smart

FIREWORKS

The evening sky is full of noise
Last night just full of stars
It's firework night for girls and boys
We usually just hear cars

The silver moon rides high tonight
As rockets reach the skies
With showers of artificial stars -
The real ones fill my eyes

It's just like World War Three out there
With bangers, silver rain,
Roll on tomorrow, Nov 6th
When all is quiet again

For every night I watch the moon
And stargaze, full of awe . . .
The beauty of the sky at night
Is silent, evermore.

Diana Price

OUR CHEMIST'S SHOP

Pot pourri and TCP, talcum and disinfectant
The baby goods section - a treasure-trove for the ladies who
                                        were expectant
Bottles and dummies, nappies and bibs, and don't forget the potty!
The perfumes of Yardley, Bromley and Tweed and that old
                                        favourite - Coty.
Mixtures for coughs, tablets for pain, lotions for spots and rashes.
Treatment for acne, and skincare advice, for the worried young
                                        lads and lasses.

An ointment we sold - we were very bold
Took care not to make a blunder
We called it 'Australian' because of its use,
It was great for discomfort 'down under'!

The days were busy, and interesting too
But 'twas the people - they made it special
We had our problems, more than a few
But laughter makes things less awful -
Like the 'Yank' who announced in a loud clear voice
That his wife was troubled with piles!
The poor lady's secret was no more - everyone knew for miles
When they went out the door, what could we say
Expect that we hoped that they'd have a 'nice day'!

From the ladies who had it 'all taken away'
And left a big void in their tummy,
To the little boy who had just a pew fence,
And wanted a gift for his mummy.

Doctors and nurses and home-helps too
Neighbours and friends and staff
There was always a hubbub and lively to-do
Many a comical gaff
They shared with us their laughter and tears
And confessed to us their worries and fears.

Our lives were made rich by much more than just wealth
We miss them, and wish them all very good health.

P Henderson

GOODBYE AND LAUGHTER

Over seas and blue skies
Never no more goodbyes
Search here, search there
Will I ever find what I've been looking for
Oh yes, over there at that old oak door.

No milk today
My love has gone away
But he will be back
Oh yes, here he comes and my son Jack
Altogether like birds of a feather
No more sorrow life so sweet
And more to the point everything's complete.

Morning break's much too soon
I can face the afternoon
Night-time laughter
I can live for ever after
Eating, drinking all day long
I can always sing my song.

Sing here, sing there
Drinking, dancing everywhere
Will my heart ever heal
Oh yes, when I make this appeal.

Pauline Millman

THE BIRDMAN OF WHITTINGTON

The Birdman of Whittington contemplates
his life as he sits all alone,
in what once was their beautiful garden,
still lovely but now overgrown.

He rests on a bench that he made long ago,
where they often would sit for hours.
If he closes his eyes he can see her,
still lovingly tending the flowers.

He has fashioned a fine new bird table
from pieces of wood he has saved,
and feels proud of his latest creation,
for several weeks he has slaved.

Now the table is finished he's waiting
for small feathered friends to arrive
at the table now laden with bird food,
the garden will soon come alive.

For today the sun shines on the garden,
the birds eat some food from his hand.
He's forgotten his lonely existence,
again he can say 'life is grand'.

Susan Guy

OUT WITH THE OLD AND IN WITH THE NEW

The good ole days, the barefoot days
They're gone but not forgotten.
It's New Year's Eve and what a treat
The mummas are out and about the street.
Black sooty faces, turbans and mum's pinnies.
Laden up with dusters we still looked like ninnies.
Knocking on doors to make a penny or two.
Dusting away old dust to make room for the new.
It was bad luck to talk so you went around humming,
Folk got shut of you quick because their nerves were a drumming.
We would laugh when some fool would knock at Mrs Hare's door
Because the crafty old devil would keep ya half an hour or more,
'Don't think ya gettin' paid, ya missed a bit!' an' towards ya
                                              she'd walk.
'Now be off wi ya ya little devils' and she'd give ya a nasty poke.
Our Bob and I not being daft rubbed our hands with a rub a dub dub,
And headed off down't street to the Britannia pub.
I looked at the landlord with my big blue eyes he wanted me in an out.
Funny thing was he offered me a shilling as I dusted the
                                              bottles 'o' stout.

I went around all tables dustin' like a whippet
And a penny or half penny you bet I didn't miss it.
Of course you'll all know it went ta best charity of all.
When wages are low and ya cannot get dole,
But better things were yet to come when Dad came home to Mum.
Mum, nowhere in sight Dad full 'o' beer made him feel very glum
We were all next door at Mrs Walkers and heard a big thud on the floor.
Mrs Walker said, 'There's burglars next door Flo, we're goin' to
                                              count to four.'
'Aye lass,' Mum said, 'I ain't got much ta tek.' Don't worry lass,
I'll be back in a sec,' said Mrs Walker, soon up from't cellar wi' a
couple 'o' tater sacks.
In on the count of four an' Dad's sprawled out on't floor looking
                                              down a crack

Crying out, 'Don't leave me Flo and fetch me kiddies back.'
My mum by now feeling very cool said, 'Get up ya silly ole fool.'
Ya don't leave a man when his chips are down an' by the way our
little mummas gained us half a crown.
And poor ole Mrs hare fell down on her luck.
When some down out mumma plastered her door knob in dog muck
Happy New Year to one and all. Sometimes justice seems to sound
To the old church bells toll.

I Smith

THAT'S POETRY

I'd like to write more poetry,
If I could find the time.
I've got all sorts of things to say,
But I can't make them rhyme!

I'd write about the things I've done,
And places that I've been.
I'd write about the way I feel,
And things I've never seen.

The people that I've known for years,
And those I've yet to meet.
The people I see every day
Just walking down the street.

The seasons that have come and gone
For years and years and years.
The people who live all alone,
Just hiding from their fears.

There's lots of things to write about.
Who cares if they don't rhyme!
So, in this busy life I lead,
I'll have to make the time!

David Hew

A BAG OF NERVES

Do we become complacent as we grow older,
Lose our naiveté, become much bolder?
Well, that's the way it would appear to me
As I recall how easily scared I used to be.

I'd read my library books on the bus going home
With no thought of the walk through dark streets to come,
And then there we were; if my book was about stalking,
With trembling legs I'd force myself to keep walking!

I remember too going home one night quite late
During the blackout, and I couldn't find the gate.
I fumbled along the railings till I was in hysterics,
But mother heard my cries and put an end to my theatrics!

With my children I'd watch the Daleks on 'Dr Who'.
Through barely-opened fingers was usually my view!
Or we'd all crouch down in safety behind the settee,
While I pretended I was only keeping them company!

Yet now we see dreadful, hideous sights on TV,
And they have no effect; they don't frighten me.
Some things I can't watch because I find them obscene,
But I just avert my head when they come on the screen.

So are we less fearful; has life made us hard?
Not much it seems has our finer instincts jarred.
We've become used to the hard knocks that life dishes out,
As our children will too in time, I have no doubt.

Marlene Allen

THE FOUR SEASONS

Nature is a wonderful thing,
When we see the grass so green,
We hear the birds, how sweet they sing,
What wonderful beauty, is ours to be seen.

The seasons change, as the months go by,
And we all face up to adverse weather,
We see all the bright flowers bloom and die,
Then in the mountains, blooms the heather.

Spring is the time for things to awake,
When flowers are beginning to bloom,
Then the summer comes, and we all take a break,
To enjoy the beauty, which all ends too soon.

Autumn comes, and leaves from the trees do fall,
We see them turning to gold,
We gain 'one hour' which is enjoyed by all,
Although the weather is turning cold.

Winter comes, and we sometimes get snow,
But we look forward to welcoming spring,
When we see all the flowers beginning to grow,
And once again, the birds will sing.

Nancy Queate

I REMEMBER

I think it's great to be alive
And think back to the age of five
I remember when Mother said,
'It's six o'clock and time for bed.'
I obeyed and climbed the stairs,
And I always said my prayers.
I was five when starting school
We sung our hymns in the assembly hall.
Fall in, fall in, the teacher cried
And very soon were side by side
We then held hands and went to class
Walking steady and not to fast
Reading seemed hard at first,
But arithmetic was even worse,
I settled down and got on well
My weakest subject, I could not spell
But teacher still thought well of me
I finished top in history.
As I grew up I did my best
But also naughty like the rest
As time went by I learnt a lot
To cross my Ts and do my dots
I tried hard, but not as yet
Had I become my teacher's pet?
Geography was pure hell
But in sport I did quite well.
By the time I had reached seven
I played up front for the school eleven.
Schooldays were great,
I had such fun
But I can't go back,
I'm eighty-one.

L Newcombe

OLD MAN TOAD

He was incensed . . . real hopping mad,
as he stared at me, his eyes so sad.

'What right had I' he seemed to say,
to give him a bath at the close of day.

'Had I no thought for his privacy,
disturbing him whilst awaiting his tea?'

'How dare I, a human, upset his rest -
using my hose to soak his vest?'

A glance, a sigh, and his body heaved,
as he looked at me, so thoroughly peeved.

So I moved away, took my hose elsewhere,
far from his cold malevolent glare

'Whose garden is this, I'd like to know,
for without water my flowers won't grow.'

'Of your own accord you came here today,
and if you don't like it, be on your way.'

'Your venomous spitting will not bother me,
for I own the hose, and will use it you see.'

'You may stay and eat slugs - please do feel free,
but cut out your anger. You don't frighten me.'

Betty Robertson

ON CONTEMPLATING OLD AGE

Am I ready for the time
   When my hair is snowy grown
   And I'm balding from the crown
Am I ready for that time -
   For though grey it's yet quite thick
   And so very long and slick
   That perhaps I'll sport a ponytail hung down

Am I ready for the time
   When my joints are stiff and lame
   And I'll need a Zimmer frame
Am I ready for that time.
   For my age I'm rather sprightly
   Can still waltz and tango lightly
   And my golf swing's getting better every game.

Am I ready for the time
   When rich food starts acid ache
   There'll be pills I'll have to take
Am I ready for that time.
   For my appetite's so good
   That I must decide which pud
   To follow up the burgundy and T-bone steak.

Am I ready for the time
   When I'm well past eighty-three
   All my travel's bus-pass free
Am I ready for that time.
   For the Jag I'll not surrender
   Slump in rocker by the fender
   I'd much rather drive to Brighton for a spree.

Roger Baker

HAPPY BIRTHDAY

Happy Birthday to our Aunt Helen
Who gave Jason the idea of putting gel on
Did you know that he would spend hours
In front of the mirror making tall hair towers
Checking his look and making sure it was cool
Before he could even think about leaving for school!

Happy birthday to our Aunt Helen
Who for seventy years has lived very well on
Her delicious home-cooked dinners and lunches
If you go to her house you'll get the munches
At Number thirty-eight as it is known
The place as long as I can remember that is her home

Happy birthday to our Aunt Helen
Who always has a lovely perfumy smell on
Her generous presents, she never arrives empty-handed
And this is the time to become quite candid
I think I can say without having a contradicter
I truly believe she's my mum's favourite sister!

Happy birthday to Helen who's also a great
Aunt to the seven Parsons grandkids - oops, make that eight
Westcliff Christmas memories are many and happy
With the odd tipple or two or possibly three
Murder and Sardines and Captain to Mate
Happy 70th Helen have a great date!

Carey Sellwood

AUTUMN 2001

I watch the leaves silently fall
Gracefully they flutter to the ground.
Reminding us of the poppies in the Albert Hall.
Listen carefully, there's hardly a sound.

Sun's rays shining through the trees,
Making a stairway to the sky
There's a whisper of breeze
In the silver birch so high.

Dew is sparkling on the grass,
Shining like jewels so bright.
A flutter of wings as the wild geese pass
A lovely sound and sight.

Autumn is here in all her glory
There's a fresh nip in the air.
Nature's pictures tell a story
With beauty everywhere.

There is much trouble in this world of ours
But beauty still abounds
Look at the birds and trees and flowers
Listen to nature's sounds.

Cicely Heathers

FRUITLESS EXCHANGE

(Sunday Times literary column . . . and others) state -
'It is not possible to rhyme words with orange or marble.

'Twas a midsummer morn on Stonehenge,
I stood waiting with a good many friends,
As the sun started to rise,
Someone yelled in surprise,
'It looks like a big round orange.'

We all stood aghast at this garble,
I thought, 'Someone is losing a marble,'
Then I said in a quip,
'If *that* orange dropped a pip,
I would rather be dive-bombed in Kabul.'

J Deekes

WHERE DO THE CLOUDS GO

Sailing through the sky, just like flotsam through the sea,
Floating onwards high, to a place not known to me.
Where do the clouds sail, day after day after day.
Do they live or die, or reform another way.
Ghosts across the sky, wistfully crossing the bay.
Sometimes they are bright and light in a happy vein,
Then change to incite, expedite threatening rain.
They seem unaware, whatso'er and so move on,
But to where, do they care where they meet or come from.
Rolling hills or dales, mountain or sea, you'll see them,
Are they just waiting for me, with such stratagem,
Don't they know, that I with my pen will capture them.
Until a verse is inspired, from those clouds admired,
Only then they can go, to that place I don't know.

Peter S Moore

Veteran's Day

My veteran car stood out in the alley,
Ready to go in the Brighton rally.
It had four square wheels and an open top;
It was hard to start it, but harder to stop.

It ran away once down Brixton Hill,
And stopped in the sea off Portland Bill.
We got out and plugged the engine with grout -
It's waterproof now except in a drought.

We found our place on the starting line,
With a crate or two of vintage wine.
The starter said, 'Ready? Off you go!'
But we couldn't start without a tow.

We flew the Thames at Westminster Bridge,
The engine as hot as an ice-cold fridge.
Belting along at eight miles an hour,
You never saw such a show of power.

We arrived in Brighton two months later,
To qualify as the world's best waiter.
The entries that year were two hundred and five,
And we were the very last car to arrive.

That was the end of the veteran car,
Which is used today as a topless bar,
Girls drink like fishes for most of the night -
Without any tops they never feel tight.

Since my rallying days are now all over,
I've bought that castle at the port of Dover.
I still miss the thrill of those Brighton runs,
And have to make do firing cross-channel guns.

K Cox

A NICE CUP 'O' CHAR

I'm chubby and brown but really quite small
But functional, life-saving, always on call
Whatever the crisis that happens along
I'm called for to bring back a smile and a song
Some use a teabag but others prefer
To put in the loose leaves and give it a stir
The cry when Mum comes in so tired and worn
With shopping so heavy she looks quite forlorn
'Do put the kettle on - let's have a brew
But warm the pot first that's the right thing to do'
When Aunty comes round to share some chit-chat
Out I come, ready, with two bags for that.
I try to cater for everyone's choice
Some like it weak and then comes a voice
'That's only water - just let it stand
Till it's almost jet black and then it tastes grand'
'Milk and no sugar' - 'No milk for me'
There's so many ways for how they like tea
It soothes away hurts and it helps when they're sad
It cheers and it warms and makes them feel glad
Put on the kettle and pull up a chair
I'm happy to serve, I'll always be there
When the family need me - they'd miss me for sure
If someone so careless dropped me on the floor
They'd realise then how much they need me
When someone shouts 'Come on - let's all have a nice cup of tea.'

Kath Barber

A LITTLE RHYME

When I think of verse it is usually rhyme,
Perhaps because it was rampant in my time.
To conjure up rhyme and put a smile on another face,
Helps to fill many folk with grace.
It is not easy to always find the right word
But at times appears suddenly like any bird.
Jot it down - for you see -
If you don't it might flee.

Betty Green

A Way, You'll Never Be

What I've seen
I hope you never see
It's shaped me
In a way, you'll never be.

I am scarred
In a place you cannot see.
I am affected
In a way, you'll never be.

I no sleep, without light
Are you not glad, you are not me?
I am frightened of the night
In a way, you'll never be.

C A Bond

MAGICAL MOMENTS

Her mind's eye vision burned so bright
No longer trapped by the darkness of night
A spell was cast and her heart cried out
Enthralled at the beauty that was all about
Her mind, her soul, her very being
How could she explain what she was seeing

A canopy glistened of pure simple white
The raindrops made patterns of silvery light
Cobwebs of trellis, silken and fine
Heather that smelled of garlic and wine
Hills that were shrouded in milken clouds
And mists that rolled like drunken crowds

But all were just imprints on the mind
Magical moments of the rarer kind.

Doris Hoole

HALLOWE'EN

Dark and gloomy is the sky,
Black and lowering are the hills
And through this mazy tangled wood
Eerily wails a wind that chills.

All steep and stony is the path,
Beneath my feet the dead leaves lie,
A crooked, pallid, waning moon
Climbs wearily up the brooding sky.

Bewildered by that ghostly gleam
I've wandered from the twisty track,
Moving like one in some dark dream
I find, in panic, no way back.

Shadows by gale-vexed branches cast
Chill my faint soul with nameless fear,
I stumble, pause and stand aghast
As weird unhallowed sounds I hear.

All through this fearful haunted wood
I've wandered in the eldritch night
I hate this darkling solitude,
I'm praying for the dawn's pure light!

Emma Kay

OH IN MY SOUL

When my heart is burning,
And my soul is yearning,
I am always learning how,
How to ask the question,
Vexed by the things we mention,
Knowing there's an answer now.

Forward ever reaching,
For the ways of teaching,
Holding each and every hand.
Hands that hold the friendship,
Words to show they meant it,
Growing into what was planned.

Oh in my soul, in my soul,
Oh in my soul, in my soul.
Like an ever-changing
Scene, our life is ranging
From the moment we are born.
Leave no room for doubt,
There is a real way out,
No time to mock and scorn.
Oh in my soul, in my soul.
Oh in my soul, in my soul.

John Cook

DARK IS THE NIGHT

The night is growing dark,
I feel the fast beating of my heart,
The stars and moon have forgotten me,
Of all my grief no one I see.
Lost forever is the light,
How lonely I'll be through the night,
With the coming wind I'll steer in sail,
I pray that I don't fail.
Please guide a while the beam's bright hour,
And not let the cruel sea devour.

Elisabeth Dill Perrin

THROUGH THE LOOKING GLASS

In Jordan's port of Aqaba
We're spending up our last dinar -
Counting out those foreign notes
For trips in little 'see through' boats.

We climb aboard - for some, a strain -
And gaze into a windowpane
That's in the bottom of the boat
To let us see things whilst afloat.

We launch the boat and leave the shore
And scan the Red Sea ocean floor
With many a long and hopeful wish
To view some multicoloured fish.

It isn't long when into sight
Come things that give us no delight -
Not darting fish and coral spires,
But cans and cups and lorry tyres.
What mind can leave such junk around
Where only beauty should be found?

A wreck and an Israeli tank
Are other items we would rank
As sad reminders of Man's plight
That we'd prefer kept out of sight.

But better things come into view
Like darting fish and coral blue,
A lovely ocean wilderness
That has survived Man's thoughtlessness.

By half past twelve we're back on land
And find a hotel by the sand
To order drinks and food to eat -
And make our holiday complete.

David Varley

RHYMES

To commence my wordy graph
I use Sir Walter's 'epitaph'

My second thought cannot be tardy
'The self-unseeing' Thomas Hardy

What fits better at number three
Than W B Yeates 'Innisfree'

Keeping the words tightly in tune
Comes Marlowes 'Amorous Neptune'

Could be lines one loves or hates
The words of Empsons 'Missing Dates'

With Shakespeare too 'tis plain to see
As with 'Under the Greenwood Tree'

Listed above are efforts fine
Pray, is there not a time for rhyme.

Alan Fisher

EVERY WOMAN'S HANDBAG (CORNUCOPIA)

You pulled me out a Polo mint
The hole of which was full of lint
Such generosity knows no bounds
I wondered how long it has been around
The bottom of your old handbag
(The thought of which just made me gag)
How long it had resided there
Wasn't really very clear
Amongst the clutter and debris
Of over half a century
Though it may well have been antique
I might have shown a bit of pique
And though I felt I might demure
At least it had the time to cure
For your next gift I cannot wait
That something past its sell-by date
A piece of pie? A sausage roll?
(Alright if you remove the mould)
Some chocolate or a tuna bake?
A yoghurt or a piece of cake?
What other treasures have you stored?
Your handbag is a Smorgasbord
Of salmonella part deceased
And always a 'moveable feast'.

John Smurthwaite

DESPAIR

Something - nothing
A ghostly hell
Life on dead wing
Empty hell.
In a dark space
Cobwebbed nightmare
Spider in lace
Beyond care.
Within a shape
Tormented air
Fragmented tape
Nothing there.
In a strange place
A Phantom breath
Freezes my face
Hard in death.

Pat Isiorho

ROSEBUDS

If I took a rosebud from its stem and placed it in cold store
Its development would be halted, it would not come out more
That little bud had potential but it had no chance to grow
But if brought to a place of warmth and light, God, His perfume on
                                                        it would bestow
If I dried a rosebud it would be, just a decoration perhaps of some kind
No texture at all like the living flower, no natural beauty I'd find
If I picked a bud before its time, it would not flourish well
With true growth lost and now so poor, it would not at a florist's sell.
But if I pick a rosebud when it's young but not quite fully mature
Give it care and attention, warmth and light, its potential can be
                                                        reached for sure
It will become what it is meant to be, perfect of detail in everyway
With shape, colour, perfume, all just right, it will give out its joy
                                                        all day.
The Christian life can be like that bud - if hastened too much it
                                                        soon dries
If left cold and dark it cannot grow, but given warmth and attention,
                                                        it thrives
It needs to experience the strength of God's love to reflect the beauty
                                                        of His grace
It needs showers of blessing which, through others, God gives -
Then that budding Christian life grows apace.

Muriel I Tate

LET'S HEAR IT FOR GRANDMAS

I'm joining the ranks of Grandma - I can't wait to share the good news.
I'll be able to buy little outfits and later on baby's first shoes.

It seems like a long time to wait yet because February's so far away.
It will all get very exciting and February 10th is the day.

They're looking through name books already and chosen a few for
a start.
They don't have a clue whether it's a boy or a girl but they've heard
its beating heart.

They all have a couple of scans now. They didn't do that in my day.
They've got two foetal-type pictures and in one it is looking their way.

So let's hear it for grandmas I'm saying. They have their part to play
it is true.
With cuddles and reading and playing, and bathing and baby-sitting too.

So where would we be without grandmas. They can spoil the children
at best.
They can hand them straight back when they're screaming and rush
home to catch up on some rest.

And grandmas have so much more patience. They're not harassed
so much don't you see.
They don't have to rush off to work now or come home in a rush
to make tea.

No, grandmas can just have the pleasure and leave all the grot
bits behind.
They don't have to change smelly nappies, though they'll change one
or two if they're kind.

So let's hear it for grandmas once more now. I'm going to be one of
the best.
And on February 10th 2002 my boasts will be put to the test!

Jennie Rippon

LOVE IS

I am the dust of which the stars are made
The violets in the dappled woodland glade
Each leaf that waits the season's call
To change its coat and gently fall.

I am the winds that scour the cosmic deep
Breath that trembles on babies lips in sleep
The voice that calms if he should cry
In every mother's lullaby.

I am there when far flung new worlds are born
The mouse that nestles in the golden corn
When bees go busy on their way
And mayfly live but for a day.

I am the sun and moon that give you light
The firefly in the summer's night
When sad hearts mourn and ask the heaven's why
I feel their pain, for there am I.

I am the key when time and life begins
The song that each and every singer sings
In everything both great and small
For I am love and love is all.

G Murphy

BATTLEFIELD

Since winter descended last November
It's been a battlefield. Remember
Mons and Passchendaele. A dreich war of attrition,
Of muddy salients, ice, wind, freezing rime,
Of trees like skeletons in fixed position,
Coffined in quartz and petrified in time,

Erect as crucifixes, silhouetted, stark,
Rooted in rock-hard soil. Encroaching dark
Kills melody, strangles the skylark's trills.
Last summer's songbirds are migratory.
But underneath this frozen calvary
Narcissi sleep, snowdrops and daffodils.

A halibut or hundredweight of skate,
I lie upon the slab, await my fate,
Dreaming of Capistrano, Hippocrene.
Warm, tender fingers dab me with incense,
Wire me for sound. My whole existence
Oscillates, flickers across the screen.

White-coated, disembodied voices sigh
About my diastole. Ever the critic, I
Resent alliteration's thump and thud:
Diseased, dysfunctional, dilated, dud.
I give them F for style, let musings yield
Up snowdrops, clustering on the battlefield.

Norman Bissett

BLACK'EAD BOB

Not long ago I got meself a job,
and I met the gaffer, a bloke called Bob,
I filled out a form and signed it with my name,
and on another I done the same,

The lads in the yard made it quite clear,
nothing but lies is all you will hear.
While I worked away in the scaffold yard,
the graft was easy and not too hard.

Now, Black'ead Bob told me a story,
of what he saw was quite gory,
when in Saudi in '72,
where tea was the only brew.

He told me about the Saudi law,
of the accused being tied to the floor,
and the people that gathered from around,
picking up rocks from the sandy ground.

They threw them at the accused,
bouncing off his head, and leaving a bruise,
a time came for the stoning to stop,
the word came from the very top.

The sheikh decided it was too inhumane,
and devised a plan to make it sane,
so he sent a man to the quarry,
who returned with a pile of rocks in his lorry.

The victim was still tied to the floor,
as the lorry backed and opened its rear door,
he raised the tipper up all the way,
and out slid the rocks and crushed their prey.

This is just one yarn that he told to me,
there's another tall tale about the sea,
his stories are so outrageous
you have to listen, because they're quite contagious.

K Delaney

NATURE'S WONDERS

Leaves floating down one by one making a carpet of red,
                                        gold and green,
Trees standing tall and naked with not a leaf to be seen . . .
The frosty glitter upon the rooftops in the moonlight glow.
Soon skies may darken and perhaps there will be snow.

A robin sings his winter song as only he can do,
Perched upon a holly tree - his bright red breast in view.
The snowflakes fall and another carpet will appear -
Upon the ground - in white - chilly winter now is here.

The voices of children playing on the pure white snow,
Riding on their sledges - see how fast they go.
Another day then dawns and the snow has almost gone,
Trees with new leaves appearing on branches big and strong.

Little creatures waking up from their winter sleep,
Snowdrops and tiny pansies up through the ground they peep.
Birds once again are nesting each with a song to sing.
Telling us that winter's gone and now at last it's spring.

Christine M Tracey

MILKY WAY

The milky way, a ribbon of stars,
A jewel to greet the eye.

Each different world, its secrets keep,
While time and space move by.

This universe of mass array,
That seems to have no end.

Can stretch imagination,
And fascination lend.

The twinkling stars that circle earth,
Are the crown upon its head.

And man looks ever upwards,
His destiny to tread.

But time and space are endless,
Man has a few brief years.

To travel through this alien void,
It could all end up in tears.

But this won't stop him searching,
His curiosity's too great.

Speeding in a rocket,
Could also seal his fate.

The beauty of the shimmering night,
Has beckoned man before,

This quest he'll keep pursuing,
Till he knocks on heaven's door.

Duchess Newman

'TWIXT SKILLET AND FLAME

She is caged, like a bird
Allowed seldom to fly
Beyond the purview
Of her master's eye;

And I long to redeem
What I know lies within
Her submissive demeanour,
To free it, but then

With a velvet hand
In a golden glove
Would I confine her
With fetters of love?

J C Fearnley

There's No Such Word As 'Can't'

One day Jo and Danny said to me,
'Mum, can you write some poetry?'
Well I said I didn't think I could,
'Try,' they said, 'you really should!'
So *here is* my little rhyme!
(It took me such a lot of time!)

Lynne Done

AT AN OXFAM SHOP

I've got a new job, one I like a lot
I help some other ladies in my local Oxfam shop.
Sometimes I'm on the counter ringing up the till
Other times I'm sorting bags working with a will
To see what folks have given us to fill our racks and shelves
We sell suits for the men and a selection of shirts
And then for the ladies we have lots of nice skirts
We can sell you a dress and a very smart hat
Or a blouse, shoes and handbag now how about that
For girls and boys we have lots of good toys
So many things to bring them joy
If you want a good book then do come our way
We've a large range to choose from out on display
If you like music we can help you there too
There is always a rack of tapes and CD's to look through
You might like a vase from our bric-a-brac shelf
So much to choose from to treat yourself
We also sell stationary, soaps, candles and packets of stamps
And even some shades to go on your lamps
Our wares are so varied so please visit us do
I'm sure we've a bargain just waiting for you
And think of the good your purchase will do
Helping the poor in lands far away
To have a better life each and every day
As they journey onwards along life's way
And if you have an hour or two to share
Please come and join us to show that you care.

S C Talmadge

LADY LUCK

Lady luck, she shineth bright,
Giveth me the will to fight,
Giveth me a chance to shine,
Let all good luck for once be mine.

Oh lady luck, I ask thee stay,
Remaineth thro' the coming day,
Be the calm within my storm,
Oh lady luck you shineth warm.

Lady luck I ask you this,
Why can't life always be bliss?
Why can't life always go
The way you planned?
Oh lady luck this life of mine,
I know I'll never understand.

Oh little ray of sunshine you,
Be forever with me do,
Remaineth always by my side,
Lady luck, thou knowst I tried.

Adrian Godfrey

EARLY MORNING LARK

Tuesday is the dustbin day
So Michael, early risen,
Clad simply in grey underpants
Wheeled bin into position.

Furtively he placed it
Neatly on he highway,
Closed the gate, tripped back to house
But found there was no entry.

Puzzled, shocked and anxious
He pushed and rattled handle,
Pondered how his exit
Could result in such a shamble.

But wicked sister, Judith,
Her self and early waker
Had spotted pant-clad figure
And planned a quick though quaker.

Gleefully she turned the key
And hid by kitchen wall,
Heard attempts to enter
Then unlocked to plaintive call

A chilled and trembling creature,
Feeling less than tough
Could have been in barer straits
If caught out in the buff.

Pat Squire

OUR ENDURING LOVE

Love came in the slow dawning
Of a far off May morning.
While the flowers bloom
On our journey to the tomb.
We let no morning promise fade
Into the evening shade
Without appreciation and praise
Of nature's beauty, in May's
Young morning, as sunbeams
Light our treasured dreams,
Oblivious to strife, the drums
Of war, the crumbs
Of the vanquished race
The tyrants sad disgrace.
Only the remembered dawning
Of that far off May morning.

T F Ryan

WARM FEELINGS

It was sunny and warm when I met her
In Brighton quite close to the sea,
She was smiling and giggling so freely
I was pleased she had stumbled on me

We clicked and adjourned for refreshment
Cold drinks and a snack were agreed,
We chatted and looked at each other
Our minds were set on a need

It seemed we were floating on air-waves
As we petted and moved on to more,
Excited, we stayed on embracing
Aware what our bodies were for

A while we lay there exhausted
Our eyes telling stories to each,
Then we stirred and moved ever nearer
To the sandier part of the beach

The day raced on reaching midnight
As we parted great friends with a kiss;
Unfolded a dream I was having
Experiencing unwedded-bliss!

Sam Royce

ON MY TENANT BLACKBIRD

In spring my tenant blackbird calls just before the dawn
Somewhere deep within my hedge he needs a nest secure
From fox and feral cat who prowl the cold March morn
Beside me, in my nest, sleeping still my paramour
Anxious not to wake her I stifle back a yawn
Outside the street is silent too soon for traffic roar
Too soon for flocks of starlings to gather on the lawn
Or for twittering sparrows to squabble round my cottage door
Just we two in the silence the new day not yet born
I hear his wings ascending to the leafless sycamore
In my head I seem to see him, though the curtains are still drawn
With head thrown back on the highest twig -
Oh! How the sweet notes soar
For three springs now he's occupied my tree
Paying his rent by singing first - for me.

Jack Ellison

UNCLE BILL

Born between the two great wars
In a time that's like no other
This honest Essex countryman
My father's youngest brother.

He says he's nobody special
But I know it's just not true
To all who have ever met him
And this my friend means you.

He was baptised 'Arther'
But to us he's always Bill
He's always been so special
And I guess he always will.

He lives in a white-washed cottage
Along the Maypole road
The lawns are neatly manicured
Flowerbeds freshly hoed.

This gentle home grown Essex man
In cap and faded shirt of blue
He nods, he smiles and shakes your hand
For his main concern is you.

Always pleased with your company
And always the perfect host
I don't know out of the two of us
Who is pleased to see who the most.

This Essex man is quite unique
For I know not of another
When he was born they broke the mould
My father's youngest brother.

K S Nunn

COPYCAT

I saw this blouse in Top Shop,
A gorgeous shade of blue.
I snaffled it up immediately -
Then my best friend bought one too!

My face turned red with anger.
A fire filled my heart.
It made my face contort itself -
A proper work of art.

'What's up?' she asked me, kindly,
'Nothing,' I replied.
(But as my face was scarlet,
I think she knows I lied.)

I told myself 'No worries!
It's just a one-off thing!'
Until the day of the disco came -
Surprise! She had my ring!

It happened once too often,
Too often for me to endure.
And when she turned up in my dress
That was the final straw!

I lost my temper there and then,
She said, 'Let me explain!'
Coincidence, me thinketh not -
She's driven me insane!

'Imitation is the finest form of flattery,'
I heard my mother say.
Well I call it damned annoying!
I'm me, let's keep it that way!

Jacqueline Howard

WOLVES AND WHALES

I hear the cry of wolves and whales
Whose rending echoes never fail
To sing of cosmic sorrow borne
In fellowship and wisdom torn
With blood and pain from sex and death
From hunger cold and panting breath
So unadorned and hauntingly
Expressed by wolves and whales; to be
Reminders we are chthonic souls;
An eerie story sadly told
With falling cadences so wild
From wolf or whale as nature's child
Articulating that which we
In our corrupt humanity
Need urgently to learn before
Their fateful songs are heard no more.

Nicholas Howard

TENDER LONGING

Year in, year out,
we dread, yet suffer.
Those long quiet nights,
without each other.
So slow and lonely,
while, always followed by.
Transparent days - compelling,
tender longing - on high.

Yet! Still it seems,
all is fate enduring.
With us to ponder; wish,
hope and wonder - alluring.

To seek, to find,
that one eternal.
Supreme - true love,
as if carnal.
While rekindling passions,
of long forgotten times.
Those tender emotions,
    - so sublime.

Gary J Finlay

THE MEETING HOUSE BURIAL GROUND 2000

I went into the burial ground because my heart was sore
I hoped that it would ease the ache - it always had before.
So many little problems had grown to super size
They kept my heart from loving, the sunshine from my eyes.
I settled down on Dora's seat to try to clear my mind
Beneath the chestnut's outstretched arms, comforting and kind.
White clouds were racing overhead, peep-boing with the sun,
And all save me was bright and gay now summer had begun.
A busy blackbird hopping by looked up and seemed to say,
'You have no business to be sad on such a lovely day,
Self pity is a sorry thing, look round and you will find
A dozen uses for your hands and solace for your mind.'
I took my little friend's advice, and looking round I saw
A host of healthy nettles that were not there before.
That grass was creeping o'er the graves where quiet lie the Friends -
One pair of hands - so much to do before the short day ends.
I fetched my trowel, my faithful friend, and promptly made a start,
And as I worked the numbness thawed and melted round my heart,
I didn't see across the grass long shadows come again,
I only knew Earth's blessed smell after summer rain.
God first made a garden when this old earth was new
And Adam was his gardener, as we His labourers too.
Though fruits of toil are blessed wise gardeners are aware
They must at last hand on their tools for other gardeners' care.

Joyce Preddle

MEMORY

The lamb? I still know Mary,
And waterproofed young John,
And rosy-cheeked Augustus,
Though they are all long gone.

And Sylvia, who was she?
Miranda at the inn,
And Timothy Winter's grandma,
Who soaked herself in gin.

The names remain to haunt me
In corners of my mind,
With London's domes and theatres,
And Wenlock Edge entwined.

'The madding crowd', 'If you can',
'I shot the albatross',
The phrases all come tumbling,
Forever safe from loss.

Well, no, I don't remember
The poems of today.
They have no key to lock them,
The poetry slips away.

I will remember only
The songs of modern time.
My simple mind retains them.
And why? Because they rhyme.

Mary Robertson

THE ARTIST

With trembling hands, his fingers curled in pain,
the old man lifted his painting - looking into it again.
His faded blue eyes, still commanding and masterly,
critically assessed the perfection of his artistry.
His mind's eye recalled details of the winter's day,
figures sharp and black, distance blurred and grey.
He remembered too, a single-minded concentration
as he committed to canvas with skill and attention
the ordinary setting, hurrying ordinary people
captured by his talent extraordinary and forceful.
Finally he sat back having studied his craft.
Had he accomplished what had been in his heart?
Half a century later -
from inspiration, to inception, then completion,
the artist knew
his heart had been true.

Sheila O'Hare

RHYME IN TIME

R   hymes are meant for you to read
H   opefully they plant a seed
Y   ou could just make someone's day
M   aybe bring a brighter ray
E   ach and every day's a gift

I   ndeed it could your soul lift
N   o one is ever on one's own

T   here's no need to be alone
I   magine friends from your past
M   emories will always last
E   ternal love knows no time.

Suzanne Joy Golding

THE LONE FISH HUNTER

An old fisherman rows into view
As if carved from Neptune's dreams
Pulls in the nets and lobster pots
And ponders a lifetime of scenes
In weather beaten bays and plots
The headland is misty it seems
As if the sea is made of blue dots
And old fish that he caught
Pass by in an old yacht
Across seas that time forgot
Mending old nets on the quay
The moon reflects off an old key
That opens the door to special dreams
To become a man of substance and means
His eyes reflect the lighthouse on a rock,
As sea birds turn and dip in a flock.

Tim Sharman

A Time For Rhyme

I like lines that rhyme on their own
Without reaching or searching for books on loan
With dictionaries and computers getting words to ring
It is not poetry if it does not swing
Even sadness and madness can be made to rhyme
Or lovely words like 'Holy' and 'Holly' mean Xmas to me
But to get the full beauty of words like 'Christmas tree'
It must be growing and rhyming in tune with thee
Without rules of grammar because poets must be free

Especially at ninety-three!

W C Pafford

GIVING BIRTH

A baby is special
A baby's in there
You can feel it kicking everywhere
But when it's time to come out
You will feel pain and give a few shouts.

You might even scream
You might even yell
But you don't care, oh what the hell
You will give a few pushes
And give a few words
But they are nothing
When you see the baby
Out of this world.

When it's all over
You are out of pain
You have one thing to he proud of
And that's what you have gained.

Gillian Tarleton

WHEN I WAS SMALL

Oh happy days so long ago
When I was very small
And all the world's a wondrous place
And Christmas trees were tall
I stayed at Granny's cottage
In the country fresh and green
She had the prettiest garden
That I have ever seen
The old black cat was purring
As she curled up on her chair
The fire bright and crackling
And warming everywhere
The table, it was laid for tea
- My favourite chocolate cake
And sandwiches of strawberry jam
My granny used to make
And from the cosy kitchen
Came the smell of home-made bread
The pretty flickering candle
To light me up to bed
The old grandfather clock
Stood gently ticking in the hall
Oh happy days when I was young
And Christmas trees where tall.

W P Davis

CHRISTMAS CELEBRATION

We celebrate Christmas in all kinds of weather
The snow falls so silent it lands like a feather
Our houses are bright from lit fairy lights
To add to the snow and the glistening nights
Holly and mistletoe we hang in the hall
We greet family and friends when they come to call
Everything is magic we enjoy lots of fun
And go to bed happily when the day is done.

Rita Pulford

EVENING

Golden sun sinks in the west
Singing birds fly home to nest,
Flowers nod tired heads to fall
Asleep on Mother Nature's breast.

Folded in Mother's wings
In nests which out of reach clings
High above among the eaves
Little birds sleep while Mother sings.

A child's evening prayer is said
On Mother's breast pillows head
Love light shining in her eyes
Mother carries her to bed.

B M Kerby

OLD FAMILIAR FACES

Those old familiar faces gone - all gone - as I sit down and stare
At ageing lines with heads of grey and white amidst dark tinted hair.
But we were young with perfect skin - we couldn't age, not then -
                                    but now
This must be imaging myself - I'm shocked to think that this is how

I too appear - inside still young - but I'm as old as all the rest
I peer a little closer - come to realise that by request
A name plan has been tucked behind to help remember who we were
Of course . . . that's Hazel Tomlinson . . . Val Watkins . . . Joy
                                    and Pat Sinclair!
But I still see them as before, in gym slips, some with braided hair
The uniform was navy blue and always we would have to wear
A beret or a Panama outside the grounds - imagine that -
I smile and smooth the photograph and let nostalgia take me back

To when the centre of my world was school - a safe and happy place
Though strict with rules you didn't bend and penalties you'd have
                                    to face.
But looking back, if boundary lines were overturned, I've no recall
Of any major upset - no one ever was expelled at all!

We had our ups and downs of course and probably we couldn't wait
To leave and spread our wings - be rid of all the pompous red
                                    school tape.
Especially, when we'd reached the sixth - elitists on some upper floor
Who claimed respect from plebs that held our seniority in awe

But having seen the world outside it's comforting to now look back
Appreciate those carefree days - the hockey pitch - the hurdles track
The sports days when our classmates spurred us on with cheers
                                    and wished us luck
And raised on high whoever won the tennis or the swimming cup

Those old familiar faces gone, forever lost - now past their prime
Look up at me with smiles that seem to be remembering a time
When life was full of enterprise and relish for the great unknown
Enticing and beguiling then, when we were barely fully grown.

Jo Lewis

THE HAMSTER

I watch the hamster in her cage,
Furiously biting the bars with rage,
She cannot scream, she cannot shout,
She cannot plead to be let out.
On her wheel she treads round and round,
But she never covers any ground,
She pushes the wheel faster and faster,
She advances not, for the cage is her master.
I wonder how she reflects on her life?
Is she happy or filled with strife?
I think in a way, she must feel like me,
Wondering if she will ever find the key,
The key to free us from our lives as they are,
To be able to run, be happy and travel far,
But for now we both imprisoned shall be,
Hoping that one day, we two will be free.

Corinda Daw

SUBMISSIONS INVITED
SOMETHING FOR EVERYONE

POETRY NOW 2002 - Any subject,
any style, any time.

WOMENSWORDS 2002 - Strictly women,
have your say the female way!

STRONGWORDS 2002 - Warning!
Age restriction, must be between 16-24,
opinionated and have strong views.
(Not for the faint-hearted)

All poems no longer than 30 lines.
Always welcome! No fee!
Cash Prizes to be won!

Mark your envelope (eg *Poetry Now) 2002*
Send to:
Forward Press Ltd
Remus House, Coltsfoot Drive,
Peterborough, PE2 9JX

**OVER £10,000 POETRY PRIZES
TO BE WON!**

Judging will take place in October 2002